BEHIND
THE
BADGE

Judy
Thank you for being
a part of my journey!

Antonette M. Jones

#3641

BEHIND THE BADGE

HER STORY

ANTOINETTE M. JAMES

Created Art Enterprises
Oak Park, MI

BEHIND THE BADGE: HER STORY

This book is based on true events. The author has tried to recreate events, locales, and conversations from memory. To maintain anonymity, the author has changed the names of some individuals and places. Some events have been slightly altered for entertainment, and some dialogue has been recreated.

BEHIND THE BADGE: HER STORY © 2021 Antoinette M. James

Paperback ISBN: 978-0-578-71061-7

Published by Created Arts Enterprises
Oak Park, MI

Printed in the United States of America
First Edition May 2021

Cover Design by: Make Your Mark Publishing Solutions
Interior Layout by: Make Your Mark Publishing Solutions
Editing: Make Your Mark Publishing Solutions

ACKNOWLEDGMENTS

I want to first acknowledge God for preparing me to write this book. I would also like to thank my grandsons, Prince, Jerald, and Eric, for encouraging Nanna with your hugs and kisses and checking in to see if I was okay. And to my husband, Anthony Robert—thank you for your love, patience, support, and late-night snacks.

Writing a book about the story of my life was a surreal process, harder than I thought and more rewarding than I could have ever imagined. Thank you to my publishing team for the editorial help, keen insight, and ongoing support in bringing my story to life. It is because of your efforts and encouragement that I have a legacy to pass on to my family where one didn't exist before.

All heroes don't wear capes. I'm forever grateful to my cousin Ray for your bravery and courage and for being a great officer along with all the men and women who serve and protect.

FOREWORD

I am super excited about this book and more elated about the author. I had the pleasure of being on a podcast with the topic of domestic violence in October 2020. Due to the pandemic, everything was being done virtually. I was asked to be a part to provide my expertise on mental health. I am known as "The People Expert" and can be seen on Fox 2 News Detroit weekly and heard on various national platforms, helping people with people. Ms. James was a guest, sharing her story, and I was mesmerized. She was transparent, raw, and relatable. The next day, she reached out to me. She shared that there were some things I'd shared that she had not even thought about before. We have developed an amazing connection.

One of the things I know is that to be a voice, you must develop your listening skills. This vessel can share and, more importantly, listen. Listening is a skill, whereas hearing is a bodily function! This book tells a story that provides the naked truth about the streets, police, and gender discrimination. Currently, in the world, we are exposed to so much pain and destruction; however, the things we do not see are so much worse. Navigating the world as a black woman has its challenges; however, add to that being extremely attractive, working undercover, and dealing with men both in the world of crime and the police world. Sadly, neither are super supportive or protective of the woman.

This story demonstrates just how difficult women, more importantly, black women have it in the world. We hear the term "breaking the glass ceiling" within the corporate spaces. This continues to be a major challenge, as men make up sixty-two percent of managerial roles while women make up only thirty-eight percent. Women earn less, are promoted less, and are penalized for caring for family. Breaking a *blue* glass ceiling is damn near impossible. Currently, out of the 100 largest cities in the U.S., only seven have African American police chiefs. So when you are female, need assistance, and only have men to turn to, too often, they stick with each other. Many do not even view the woman as someone who should be wearing the uniform.

Although the systems are vastly different from the street code to the police code, when it comes to how they treat women, there are lots of similarities! Even the church demonstrates a disregard for women. The story reveals a pastor who was soliciting a prostitute and was able to call on the mayor and police chief to sweep away the issue. So from the pimp to the politician, to the pastor, and finally the police, there is nowhere for the woman to turn.

Buckle in, get your favorite snack and beverage as you get ready to be taken on a ride that will have you biting your nails and holding your breath. I am sure that *Behind the Badge,* there are many stories ... but not quite like *Her Story*!

Dr. Sabrina Jackson
"The People Expert"
www.sabrinajackson.com

NOTE FROM THE AUTHOR

Detroit would be the place where I journeyed to live a dream ... only to become the main character in a reality show, not the *Preachers of Detroit* but the show called Life. In writing my journey, I would be told by the editor multiple times that I needed to go deeper ... dig into the crevices of my soul and pull out the "stuff." Be transparent. That's essentially what I was told. "Readers want to be touched and moved by your story. You want them to imagine themselves in your world and situations that test them. Let the reader feel, see, taste, and touch."

So, there I was ... back at the drawing board ... and multiple times. It would take me multiple times to get it right, right? And I did. I believe I got it right. So thank you for taking this journey with me. It was a privilege to share my story and introduce you to my life behind the badge as well as my relationship with my daughters, who were inspirational during my growth in life. It was through them that I learned the real power of faith, hope, and love. I hope I've given you the courage to unpack your own stories.

I resigned from the department and won my worker's compensation claim. At the advice of my legal counsel, I did not take my sexual harassment claim to trial. But I still prevailed, nonetheless. Through all I have been through, God has shown me that he was preparing me all my life for such a time as this and that there is a time, season, and purpose for everything!

The people who leave an impression on my mind are not the ones I would have imagined. They're not your average city residents; the most resilient, inspirational individuals are teenagers, including my own daughters, who persevered and made it through one of the most pivotal moments in their lives. I extend a special thanks to all the young people at the Lansing Boys & Girls Clubs and the Safety Station. The Robert Ray Jr.'s, the Dominiques, Adrians, etc. Thank you!

My story as a Detroit police officer was no accident. No chance or happenstance. It had to be God. My journey in life is not something you can make up. It's just something I had to experience so I could know. Something I could only *know*. It comes to you at times like a light through the tunnel to show you the way.

Out of the blue skies, a family of clouds exist ... the dust of Jesus' feet. The picture in the sky doesn't lie. We are all here for a purpose—our destiny. And God *does* exist. He spies with his wise eyes. He speaks so clearly with a truth so clear that people's ears itch for a different message. And just like that, one day, God showed me that I didn't need to search for the answers because they were already within me, in both the good times and the bad times. In the tragedies and triumphs. Every experience was meant to awaken me to another level. Each moment in life contains a message, offering detailed guidance and connecting the dots.

For my three daughters, thank you for being my
purpose and inspiration. I love you.
and
My identical twin sister and big brother—I wrote it!
and
Mom, thank you for believing in me!

INTRODUCTION

I am a former police officer for the City of Detroit Police Department.

"Bet you've seen it all" is the response from many when they learn of my past profession. "What was it like to be a Detroit cop?" "Have you ever been shot at?" And the comment that really gets the Oscar award for famous female cop line—"You are too pretty to be a cop ... You look like a schoolteacher!"

I began my career as a thirty–one-year-old woman, like anyone else who has dreamed of being a police officer—with hard, tough training at an academy ... the Detroit Police Academy

I guess for those who sit at home watching crime stories, whether its *C.S.I.*, *The First 48*, *911*, or *The Shield*, one might wonder whether being a cop is portrayed accurately on television. The excitement of the nonstop action, not to mention the weightlifting-type male cops who answer a police officer run to a domestic violence encounter that turns into, "Baby, here's my phone number" from the damsel in distress. What you see on television is so close yet so far from reality that you can never really understand it unless you've been there, done that. Forget all the illusions on television and lies police recruiters sell as having "required characteristics." The realities of making split-second decisions could mean life or death. This was a constant truth.

As a Detroit cop, it was a constant irritation for me for the duration of the five and half years I was in the police force, from the criminals' responses at arrest: "You can cuff me any day," to civilians, which included family, who questioned my sanity. At the same time, several colleagues were consistently asking to date me, be it a relationship or a one-night stand. Being on the force required more than being brave; it took trusting your instinct and knowing the people you served to protect and the ones you worked with, but above all, it meant protecting yourself.

Twelve precincts are nestled throughout Detroit's cluster of neighborhoods. Some of the officers walked the beat; others patrolled the streets in uniform, and hand-selected officers worked the 30 Series, a specialized unit within the precinct that worked undercover to put out the small fires of crime in that precinct's area. And then there were the citywide units that covered the city's crime centered crisis from Narcotics, to Vice, Homicide, Crime Scene Investigations, and everything in between.

Detroit is an island of hidden treasures of various ethnic cultures and jewels expressed through authentic cuisine—Xochimilco Restaurant in Southwest Detroit's Mexican Town had the best nacho supreme and margaritas. The Westside was notorious for Theresa's delicious fried perch, French fries, and peach cobbler. And downtown was known for Floods Bar & Grill, where sounds of live jazz enhanced a soul food platter of collard greens, candied yams, and mac & cheese. The Eastside was home to Bert's Marketplace, where the smell of ribs saturated the air as jazz music echoed for blocks. And if you gotta have art, Detroit Art Institute, Charles H. Wright, and the Motown Museum shared history in culture and music. Neighborhoods scattered throughout the city experiencing high crime, involving drugs, prostitution, auto theft, gangs, and gun violence, had an increasing number of homicides. They were called hot spots.

Each police precinct was a community within itself, with different requirements of its personnel. Specialized Units had their own identity. Located off the river, officers patrolled downtown attractions, hotels, and clubs, and directed traffic for significant sporting events and concert venues. You had to be clean to be selected for this detail, have a high-gloss shine on your shoes, and wear a crisp uniform adorned with military creases.

Straight from the academy, cops were assigned to precincts despite being asked to submit a wish list for their top three units. Homicide, Crime Scene Investigation, and Vice were my selections … and in that order. I had no intentions of working the streets too long. Still, a select few were chosen for a specific detail—Atwater or headquarters, which was crowded by the department's top brass, where story-hungry news reporters camped out, waiting to interview for an investigative story, which were considered dream assignments. The Atwater detail was for the hand-selected cops whose faces represented the department's esteemed profession or those too scared to patrol the streets and brown-nosed to walk the beat.

I've been told by strangers that being a cop is great work, serving and protecting citizens while putting my life on the line every day. Family, friends, and associates' comments were sarcastic about my job. From "Here comes 5-O" or "Hide the marijuana!" if they lit up a joint at the backyard summer parties. As a rookie, "Mind N Our Business" was the slogan created by Jerry Oliver, the former Detroit Police Department chief, who was also the mayor's family. It created confusion amongst the citizens and City Council, who stated that the button was inappropriate, grammatically incorrect, and delivered the wrong message about the police. Rumor had it that the City Council emailed the chief questioning the "our" in the slogan, whose "business" was Detroit's police handling, and why the money was being spent on buttons instead of hiring more officers.

As officers mandated to wear a button used as a positive message to the citizens, we kept our minds on policing. It went beyond being community-friendly cops against robbers who just lock'em up and throw away the key. Did the City Council not know that the police chief led the force outside of the mayor and had the final authority on all policy-related issues? Well, it wasn't true in every situation, and I would soon fall prey to the underworld of law enforcement that ran deep.

Being an African American female police officer, what may have appeared to the public as prestigious police duty was more brown-nosing than police work. The high-crime areas, from 48205, covering the Ninth Precinct—listed as the most dangerous zip code in our country—to the Eighth Precinct and every precinct in be-tween, were combat zones, where cutting off body mics and throw-ing them in the glove box and cutting off the cameras on police runs were shared practices across the entire department.

While the department was a culture within itself, each precinct, each unit, and leadership level followed its own rules, and each pre-cinct and unit came with its own practices and traditions. Each also had its own subculture and secret language. A code of silence, where snitches were bitches, extended beyond the 'hood, through the veins of law enforcement. Police, preachers, and politicians, together, were the real cops and robbers, covering each other's backs.

The only time reporters showed up on a scene was to cover a

story on the latest newsworthy homicide, or a dirty-cop-turned-dope man, who was busted on a drug deal, or police brutality by the "Botty Boys," who earned the nickname due to suspected illegal body cavity searches.

We all love the good guys, right? But what happens when you finally arrive on the scene and discover there's a whole different set of rules, other than the ones they preached like a Sunday morning sermon in the academy? No one's playing fair out there—not even your brothers in blue—and you must shift your mindset accordingly. All the clear-cut, black-and-white concepts of right and wrong that you're taught all your life start to bleed together, except I believed there were shades of gray that shifted from absolutes into straddling the fence.

"Throw that academy training shit out the window" would become a theme for seasoned officers I worked with on every shift at every precinct. The uniform is open to perceptions, excluding the bulletproof vest, like a life jacket to a boater. Most of us recruits started out equipped with determination, some with a fear of death, wearing our code of ethics as if it were our Glock, sure to conquer the city's evils.

We were trained to be "RoboCops"—catch the bad guys, help the oppressed, and maintain truth, justice, and a perfect life. Forget the sarcastic macho and butch soldier types, the ones who think the badge gives them a license to harass, shoot, and kill. Boots on the grounds, hitting the streets, a rookie, self-confident in what's real, what's right. One month into the job, and you begin to question. One year later, you're lost like Dorothy in *The Wizard of Oz*, wanting to go back home.

My enlightening life did not begin in the classrooms of college or on the first day of being a police officer. It goes back to when I was a kid. My heroes were from TV shows; from the screen to reality, the characters seemed to have all the behind-the-scenes secrets, the inside scoop during their endless investigations to solve crimes and cold cases. To me, they seemed to be at the center of all the major trials; I have watched them all. The hidden knowledge of the world was at my fingertips.

There are questions that will obviously come from those who know me, worked with me, and even hopefully from my readers, who will become familiar with me by turning the pages of this book. Are the people real? Did the events described here really occur? Was I personally involved in the events described? The answers to all these questions are yes and no. Are the other people shown here real? Yes, of course, they are, but there is no individual in this book, including myself, who has been betrayed based on someone I have come to know or have been associated with.

All the events described in this book are real. I've been the main character in my own Lifetime story, a big-screen film that has allowed me to obtain inside information. For one reason or another, each person represented merely serves as the means by which the story must be told.

The events are not of their own making, and since the stories are true, they are combined with an essential knowledge of the female police officer, and I feel it is my obligation as a writer to be discerning, to go back in time to bring it forward, to build, outline, and shape my story for the purpose of awakening in such a manner to reveal what I have found to be the truth.

As the writer, there's no need to provide clarification, to some degree. Yes, I was, as any police officer, self-motivated and a team player, part of the brotherhood, weaving life experiences and my emotional understanding of events that is the fabric of this book.

The things that happened to me before becoming a police officer and the things that happened, not just to me, but also to other police officers during my law enforcement career provide an extraordinary chance for the reader to sit and listen and connect the stories as they were registered. I was a police officer who understood them. Perhaps this is why the book was written, to show you the inside and outside world of being more than a police officer, an African American female police officer.

One thing for sure, being a police officer was a journey. Staying alive, maintaining my sanity, the ability to laugh, and prayer were all crucial and essential for survival. Hanging to the last shred of hope that there are some good people out there, which was a challenge when encountering evil every day. I was going to be a superhero! Super Mom and Super Cop to shine for all the world to see that I had finally made it. A black female cop, single mother of three daughters, patrolled Detroit's streets—from uniform to working undercover. Being hand-selected for the Executive Protection Unit for the mayor's wife and three sons and hands-on training for Crime Scene Investigation was no easy feat.

My life had moments of heartbreak and happiness, danger and calamity, weird humor, and situations so unbelievable that a layperson would attest that they were out of a Hollywood movie. I am here to tell you they were real in more ways than one.

The training was intended to turn my classmates and me into the police and be a part of a family that would become the enemy.

Antoinette James, former police officer, Detroit Police Department

The greatest gift our parents ever gave us was each other.

April 10, 2002: My graduation from the Detroit Police Academy,
Class 2002- D. (L to R - My twin, Bernadette McClair, me, and my
brother, Carlitos Bosti)

CHAPTER

1

WHAT'S DONE IN THE DARK

I t was a chilly early April evening in Detroit when I became aware that the code of silence within Detroit's law enforcement—a legend within its subculture that extends beyond the badge—might have a fatal outcome. I had foolishly believed I was safe.

Crime in the city was high, and so were the citizens' complaints on drugs and prostitution. Everyone in the station automatically knew, as though a sounding of an alarm had been triggered. A city-wide, offer to engage vice sting operation (O.T.E.) was activated in the precinct for the night.

"Chyna, you're the decoy for the night," Lieutenant Dan announced during the 6:45 PM roll call. It was time to go undercover.

"Ten-four, Lieutenant Dan," I replied. Heading down the hallway to prepare for my shift duties, I reached into my backpack, pulled out my headset, and turned on R. Kelly's "Bump and Grind," which helped me mentally prepare for the night and transform into my alter ego. I approached the dressing room, thinking to myself how amazing this hideaway hub they called the "Bat Cave" was. The Bat Cave was camouflaged within Detroit's abandoned industrial decay, nestled and carved in the cemented structure that housed the Vice and Narcotics units, a secret hideout just blocks away from the Eastern Market, the morgue, Detroit Receiving Hospital, and Downtown Detroit.

I walked over to my locker to search for my outfit of the night. I sifted through my bag of costumes, wigs, and shoes. "Showtime for the number one hooker of the streets," I whispered under my breath as I applied the final touches of makeup. And yes, I was just *that* good. I admired the provocative white shorts, tank top, and jacket, with stiletto boots that laced my long, lean, shapely 5'10" frame.

It was time to go undercover.

Sugar, Stone, Young, and Drake were the takedown arresting officers in squad cars as Lieutenant Dan and Sergeant Salt tailed them in their unmarked silver, window-tinted Grand Prix.

We hopped into the backseat of our unmarked gray, rusted minivan. Tiger was the driver, and Black was his sidekick. Vice caravanned to the westside. Black was the eyes for the night, fitted in blue jeans that were torn and mudded, a grease-stained grimy shirt, and tattered shoes. He was dressed like a bum, blending in with the streets to watch out for me. Both Tiger and Black were lookouts. So when the john made a sexual proposition and offered the pay, they were the eyes to alert the crew that I got the case.

"Chyna, are you ready for the time of your life?" Tiger asked, his eyes scanning me from top to bottom. "I bet your father would be happy, seeing you have a job that lets you dress up like a hooker."

"Yeah, I bet he would! And my mama would be proud to know I was arresting pervs like him too," I shot back.

Working Vice, you had to have a sense of sexual perversion, because the jokes were utterly disgusting. But I learned to sometimes laugh nervously and roll my eyes. You'd think my response and actions would be clear, showing my disapproval, but like clockwork, Tiger started to rationalize his statement. "*Relax*, it was just a joke."

"Ready as ever." I thought Tiger was just a drop in the bucket in an entire male-dominated organization called to protect and serve, carrying a badge and a gun but making sexist jokes and engaging in other forms of harassment as well as an underworld code of silence. I was irritated, fired up, and set to catch the nightcrawlers.

"What's your code that you have the case?"

"I'll pull on my ponytail."

★　★　★

The sidewalk was my runway as I strolled, pivoted, stood, and paced the corners, waiting for strip club regulars, partygoers, and anyone else who was looking for a date.

"You wear it well; I'd pick you up myself!" Black crooned from across the street.

"I wear it better than well!" I hollered back. I was dressed in a white miniskirt, halter top, white patent leather baby doll pumps with a bedazzled bag to match, white fishnet stockings, and I was swinging a long, black wig that I wore in a ponytail. Black was fine, with Morris Chestnut fitness and smooth chocolate skin, white teeth, and glistening lips; he reminded me of a Big Boy's hot fudge ice cream sundae. Yummy.

Minutes later, a red Mustang slowly rolled across the street from the corner where I stood on display, occupied by one black male,

3

waving and beckoning for me to come. I scurried to the passenger side as he rolled down the window.

"Hello." I girlishly giggled while adding hot pink lip-gloss to my lips.

"You dating?" asked the handsome young man dressed in Detroit Pistons gear, from his baseball cap to his jersey, even wearing a gold blinged-out Detroit Pistons watch that shined in my eyes, almost blinding me. He looked young enough to be my son, with a teddy bear nose and a clean-shaven boss baby face. Tommy Hilfiger cologne and tequila wafted from the car; he must have taken a bath in them. I had a nose like a hound; plus, I loved the scent of both.

Maybe he's been at the game or just left the bar, I thought.

"What you charge? I don't have that much cash on me," he said as his pretty brown eyes beamed with excitement. Beads of sweat radiated lust and desire. His long-fingered hands fluttered nervously through the air, endlessly motioning for me to get into his car.

"It's whatever," I replied.

"You sure you ain't no cop?" he said, shifting his eyes to the rearview mirror. There was no sign of the police, no cars, and no traffic in sight. The john thought the coast was clear. He shook his head and laughed.

I stepped back from the car, winking my eye, "I ain't no cop," I said, licking my lips simultaneously.

"Hey, how about some head for five dollars?"

Jackpot! He took the bait. I had a feeling he would.

As I pulled on my ponytail, flashing lights and sirens of police cars came scurrying from all directions. Takedown, in full uniform, swooped in for the arrest.

"Out the car; hands up!" commanded Sugar, Stone, Young, and Drake simultaneously as if they were in a quartet. Before the poor john knew what was happening, he was cuffed, and his car was towed away.

Eleven down and one more to go. Twelve was our quota for the night.

Working Vice, most times, was an eight- to twelve-hour shift, from dusk 'til dawn. Pretending to be a prostitute was like being in a play, and I was the main attraction. I dressed up, changed sets, and used the streets of Detroit as my stage. I broke records for the number of impounds and arrests. Men and women of all races, no matter the marital or economic status and occupation, prowled the streets searching for a quick sex fix like a drug addict waiting to shoot heroin into their veins.

I watched people from all walks of life engage in sexual behaviors, some who were caught right in the act, risking their experiences with the threat of HIV/AIDS and other sexually transmitted infections on the horizon.

After every shift, I thought of how selfishness impacts one's health and their wives, husbands, significant others, or secret lovers without a care, no matter the cost. Addiction, be it drugs, sex, or anything in between, has no respect for anyone because what was done in the dark would eventually come to light. I was a witness to its truth.

The hour was getting late. "Chyna, we need just one more to make our quota. Just one more," Black announced.

"One more?" Not okay. I didn't want to spend another minute parading on the streets; I wanted to be home with my girls. Nicole, Marie, and Yvette were my three cubs.

"You can get us one more john, Chyna; I know you can!"

I pulled open the van door. People sauntered by whistling, and they dispersed as I strolled back onto the dark city streets. Considering

I'd been working Vice for more than a year and was no stranger to the streets of Detroit, I chalked my nervousness-slash-funny feeling up to the fact that I'd been working long hours and was worried about my relationship with my daughters.

A horn beeped and a white SUV with tinted windows slowly drove by. A man peered out the passenger window. I slung my purse over my shoulder and swung my ponytail to the side, my eyes on the passenger. He turned. My eyes and his gaze met. He pointed a finger, dropping his thumb like a gun and sped off. The car's tires spun, spitting gravel as the vehicle careened onto the road.

"Did he just do that?" A strange sense of déjà vu gave me the chills, or maybe it was the early-morning breeze. *Have I been here before?* Shaking it off, I strolled back to the corner, doing a double-take, looking again over my shoulder. It all seemed familiar yet not all at once. It was coming to me in bits and pieces.

It was getting late, and my aching feet hurt in those stiletto heels.

"It's time to take a break," I said, waving and yelling out to Black, who stood across the street from me. To random people who may have been watching, it looked like a whore screaming and waving to a bum. I was walking through the dark alley just as it started to rain. I climbed into the front seat of our unmarked gray minivan for a power nap when light filled the entire van … white, blinding light somewhere, rolling straight for us. At that moment, I couldn't see anything.

POP, POP, POP, POP!

Suddenly, I heard multiple thundering shots. They were so close and bone chilling. Four rounds shattered the glass of the passenger car window, sprinkling the street with glistening shards. Pain shot through my head; warm blood began to drip down my cheek. My left eye wouldn't focus.

The horror on Tiger and Black's faces signaled I was in trouble. "Oh, shit! Call nine-one-one. Officer down! Officer down!" Tiger screamed.

I was trying to focus, but my vision was blurred as the glare of flashing red and blue lights glimmered on my face. The takedown crew controlled the crowd. Lieutenant Dan and Salt were paralyzed with fear as they surveyed my injuries. Their eyes were full of shock.

"Drake, let's put Chyna in the back of your car!" Lieutenant Dan shouted. The scene was chaotic, with piercing sirens and thunderous sounds of doors opening and closing as the takedown crew rushed my marred body to Detroit Receiving Hospital. Things were happening quickly.

"Female officer down! She has multiple gunshot wounds!" yelled Lieutenant Dan as the medical team sped through the emergency entrance, placing my limp body on the stretcher. In the blink of an eye, it was 1995—University Towers, Wayne State University Student Housing, my daughters in tow. My journey to Detroit, chasing my dreams. Life was unlocking a floodgate of memories, like spending Christmas time with family, watching as the girls opened gifts from under the tree, or the summer weekends we spent splashing at Rolling Hills Water Park.

Is this a dream that turned into a nightmare, or am I …

In a flash, I was rushed through two tall steel doors into a room full of light. My limp and blood-soaked figure appeared lifeless. Blue scrubs and white coats were scrambling and swarming around me from all directions. Clothes sliced in half, my white outfit was now velvet red. Was I dying? Was it my time to go?

"She's bleeding profusely from four gunshot wounds; hit once behind the left ear, once through the jaw, and once through the left arm and chest!"

"Intubate her!"

"Blood pressure's falling!"

I could see and hear the panicked hospital staff, their faces flashing and diminishing, their voices fading in and out as the trauma team tirelessly worked to save my life. "Pulse is faint … Her breathing is erratic," another yelled.

I felt my chest tightening and my lungs filling up with air. I was suffocating and drowning at the same time. I was fighting to breathe.

"Jesus, we're losing her. She's going into cardiac arrest!" I watched my body shake violently. I watched as it took three staff members just to hold me down.

The smell of death saturated the air.

Oh God, I thought, *my girls!* A feeling of desperation began to overcome me. I found myself at home, Nicole standing under the hallway light, crying uncontrollably and screaming, "Mama, Mama!" *Did she have a nightmare?*

Onward to the den; Marie was passed out on the sofa. Her fingers were blue; her skin was pale. *I have got to get her to the doctor!* I thought.

"Call nine-one-one!" I screamed … but no one could hear me. *Will she be all right?* Then a loud crash of glass shattered. I ran to the kitchen. Yvette had dropped a bottle of my Vineyard Cabernet Sauvignon wine. *What was Yvette doing with my one-hundred-dollar bottle of wine? Maybe she was confused between my bottle and her Ocean Spray grape juice.*

Immediately, I was pulled back into the emergency room. In the distance, there was a black handgun that looked like a Glock, handcuffs, pepper spray, and a Detroit Police badge that had fallen to the floor into the sea of pooling blood. I hovered closer, only to see the last number on the badge—it was 0; my badge number ended in 1.

But if this wasn't my badge number, was this really me lying on the hospital bed? As I tried to figure out what was going on, I was near the ceiling, looking down and able to perceive that I was in two places at the same time. I was separated physically and spiritually—in one place but still having the knowledge and perception of the body in another. My vision now was nothing like it had been before. It was utterly like I had gone back in time in a mystifying dimension, like Dr. Who on a different level.

Time had stalled, and my surroundings went eerily silent. Suddenly, I realized I was outside of myself, seeing life through another dimension. I was out of my body, what they call an out-of-body experience.

Memories began unfolding like parts of a movie—images and scenes borrowed and spliced. I woke up from that dream, puzzled.

You see, I had lost years of journals that were a map for writing this book. "Maybe God is telling you to write your story differently" were the words from Venus, a published author and sister in Christ.

I asked God what the dream meant, and clear as day, I heard, "She didn't live to tell her story, but you did!" The dream was also a warning to me that questioning reality, perceptions, and legalities of what I saw from behind the badge were a war against my mental sanity, my family, and my own life. I had to learn to trust my first mind and write the book as it was given to me.

This book was not written for perfect people. This book was written for those who are trying to figure out life's journey and help them connect the dots. I pray that what I have lived through over the past fifty-one years, instead of being a light at the end of the tunnel, will be a light through the tunnel in their journey.

CHAPTER

2

WHEN I GROW UP

Growing up with a cousin in law enforcement was exposure to a career path that I always knew would be mine one day. God, he was fine. Cousin Ray. I can remember him like it was yesterday. He was tall, handsome, physically fit, wore shiny black boots with his crisp blue uniform, serving the Inkster Police Department during an era when substantial racial inequalities existed openly in policing and the criminal justice system.

I vividly remember those summer moments visiting my grandfather's house when Cousin Ray, in full uniform, would pull up in his police car to visit my grandfather, who'd be sitting in the garage. He would share his cop stories with my grandfather of walking the beat, patrolling the streets, working undercover in Narcotics, and investigating murders, all while my grandfather would remain engaged as he'd sip on beer and eat Colby cheese and crackers. I would hide behind big black garbage cans and secretly listen.

From birthday parties to backyard barbeques, Thanksgiving, Christmas, or Easter, Cousin Ray didn't miss the seasonal family gatherings or holiday dinners. Sometimes alone or with a partner, faithfully, he'd stop by in uniform, his badge shinning bright, and strapped to his side was a big black gun. During those moments, he didn't talk about the fear, anxiety, or distress of the job; he came to fellowship, laugh, and break bread. But it was often short lived because moments later, we'd hear … *"Fifteen dash six … a person with a weapon. Caller states neighbor threatened to shoot him, brandishing a black handgun,"* emanating from a female dispatcher's crackled voice over the police radio.

"Fifteen dash six en route. Requesting back up," Cousin Ray would respond. And just like that, he had to go without having had a chance to eat.

I didn't understand how he returned to a dangerous job, risking his life daily, being shot at, injured, called nigger, or spat at in the face. But then there were the stories of triumph, of rescuing cats from trees and women and children from abuse, mentoring troubled boys out of the gang- and drug-dealing life, to comforting and calming those at homicide scenes or even buying the elderly groceries while at the store.

I guess those little things made it worthwhile, recalling the funny stories, the crazy ones. But there were dark memories that time will never erase, like the Summer of 1987 when three Inkster police [A40] officers, my cousin's fellow officers, who were serving a bad-check arrest warrant on a woman and her sons at the Bungalow Motel, were tragically shot and killed. Cousin Ray cried that day, when his department, the community, and brotherhood grieved such a tragic loss. After that day, I knew one thing for sure; at any given moment, he might be the one who wouldn't make it home.

Like so many others, Cousin Ray adjusted, learned how to wear the mask that matched his shield. As a cop, I had a close-up view of how and why a cop was viewed as a superhero. We saw Cousin Ray that way. It came with wearing a bulletproof vest, carrying a gun, fighting to catch the bad guys, and not caring about the applause or rebukes or any negativity from others. No matter what happened, they knew they had a duty to serve and protect the community without expecting anything in return.

Having a cousin as a cop gave me a close and personal look into the lives of those in blue. I wanted to do the same, not for Inkster but for Detroit.

At the tender age of seventeen, I learned through his stories that being a police officer was dangerous, that answering a run or delivering a warrant could be a matter of life or death.

Thank you, Cousin Raymond, for your seventeen years of service.

* * * *

From the day we're born until the day we die, people think they know our story before we even tell it. All good things must come to an end, but I didn't know that I would soon witness a vicious tsunami of shame, anger more quickly, and that calamity would introduce itself to me.

If you've ever lived any part of your life in a small town, you might relate to my credence that it is an endless love–hate relationship. I grew up in Ypsilanti, Michigan, a small town where I found myself going through a vicious cycle of finding one reason to love it and two more reasons to hate it.

We were sandwiched between two icons—Ann Arbor, home to the Big House, University of Michigan, where my brother Carlitos dreamed of one day being a college football player, and Detroit, which was forty-five minutes east, home of Motown and the 1967 Riots.

I was born as what they called an identical mirror twin—I am the youngest by six minutes—and we have two brothers, one with whom we share the same parents, and the other by way of my dad's first marriage. I was a daddy's girl.

What was the worst part of living in a small town? First, let me start by sharing what was the best. Everyone knew everyone. We were either family by blood or relation, whether through marriage, church, or being neighbors; there was no such thing as six degrees of separation. My grandparents, great aunts, uncles, cousins, and friends lived blocks from each other. From Burton Court to Ainsworth Circle, I could walk from the back door of one relative's home and into the front door of another relative's home.

If you wanted the best cheeseburger in town or to play arcade games and buy all the penny candy and snacks, it wasn't McDonald's or Chuck E. Cheese; it was Swanson's Burgers and Al's Pinball Shop, which were situated across the street from our townhouse. Not only that, but school—Perry Elementary, K-6th grade—was a hop, skip, and a jump away. It was so close that our complex was named Perry School Apartments.

To be a kid meant playing with the neighborhood crew, from king of the mountain or tackle football—I could run the ball, touch down, and score—jax or marbles on the front porch, hide-n-seek, and what time is it, Mr. Fox? We were the Little Rascals of Perry School Apartments.

When on punishment, staying indoors and being confined to my room was the sentence that reminded me of a prison cell, only to look out on the yard as friends played and laughed until dark. And during the winters, it was ice skating figure eights, sled riding until your fingers were numb from the cold, and hot chocolate to warm up our chilled bones. We didn't get to watch cartoons on Saturday mornings. It was house chores—dusting, vacuuming, laundry, or grocery shopping at Meijer with Mom, my twin, and grandmothers. I couldn't wait to ride the penny horse or have a scoop of vanilla ice cream on the cone. No matter the season, we knew to be home when the streetlights came on.

We were taught to respect our elders, from our house to the community and church—aunts, uncles, grandpas and grandmas, parents' friends, to the next-door neighbors. We took care of one another; we were like the corner convenience store where you could run across the way and get free eggs, butter, or milk without worrying about paying anyone back—we were family! I didn't want them telling my mom I'd misbehaved because she'd give me a beating twice, one for them and one for her.

And how can I forget the church and the funeral home? We'd walk a path from our backsliding patio door that led to Messiah's Temple, the little white church seated on a hill at the corner of Monroe. And Lucille's Funeral Home, the resting place for everyone in Ypsilanti who was black and died. While one was lifesaving, the other signified an end to life. Both would impact the crossroads of my life's journey.

My dad was an only child, raised by a single mother, who tragically lost her husband, his father, to a tragic hit-and-run accident in Inkster, Michigan one summer night. As a high school all-star athlete in football and track, my dad earned the nicknames "Bread" and "Bookie" for his speed and ability to catch a ball.

He was a man who was into the latest designs and fashions. He was the Billy Dee Williams from *Lady Sings the Blues*, with his brown eyes, boyish smile with pearly whites, and a mustache that would tickle my face when he kissed me goodnight. My dad's black hair was like wool. He wore a press and curl, a heavy mustache and beard trimmed to perfection, leather and velvet jackets, wide-collar shirts, creased pants, and polished shoes. He smelled like Old Spice, and he was serious about his appearance and ours too.

"You should be in Hollywood" was the cheer from all those he'd meet. "When you make plans, life happens," he shared. As a family man, he had dreams and aspirations of getting out of Inkster, Michigan and one day being an actor—rich and famous. He was the type of perfectionist who was hooked to having everything done without mistakes. It had to be perfect.

My dad was the family's interior decorator of our home. What one may have called the projects was our palace—a three-bedroom apartment in the Perry School Projects. It was colorful; the walls became dad's blank canvas. The living room was painted a deep ocean blue, and we had white fur carpet, mirrored tables, silver, and glass lamps to accent the family's first-floor model R.C.A. color television. We were rich. Our kitchen was a canary yellow with a white kitchen dinette set with matching yellow cushions, accented by yellow curtains, adorned with brown leaves.

On Sundays, he'd take us to church faithfully. We visited many churches of various denominations, from the Kingdom Halls of Jehovah's Witnesses to the hardwood pews of the Catholics, Baptist, Apostolic Pentecostals, and the Church of God in Christ. Who doesn't celebrate birthdays? Who prays silently? Who rocks to soulful hymns and police dress code violations while emotionally and physically engaging in expressions infused with chanting by way of crying loudly, "Thank you, Jesus!" repeatedly or running around the church wildly as if they were in a trance? From one extreme of religion to the other, it was like my dad was on this treasure hunt for salvation. But the best part about Sundays was dinner; without fail, we ate at Big Boy on Michigan Ave in Dearborn. Something about seeing that Big Boy with a big smile and holding that double-decker hamburger with the special sauce was the best.

My dad was fun and silly at home and visited us on his afternoon lunchbreak from Ford Motor Company, touting a bag of golden hot McDonald's French fries for a treat. In the evenings, he shared stories of monsters like vampires, werewolves, or Blackula, only to chase us upstairs howling, "I'm going to bite your neck" before putting us to bed. I ran, laughed, and cried. It was a thrill but scary at the same time. Then came the Bostic belch training.

"First, you take a deep breath," he shared as he inhaled, sucking in the air. Suddenly, he made this roaring belching sound, sort of like a lion roaring in the jungle. "That's how it's done." He chuckled. It was a long, loud, and roaring belch, so powerful we could feel it shake the house. "Now, let's see who can belch the loudest." My dad stared at each of us.

First, my brother did his.

"Good one, Carl," my dad cheered. "Little mama, you're next," he'd say. Then it was my twin's turn. She did her best shot to imitate the sound.

"That's all right, little mama. Next time," he'd say as he patted her on the back.

Finally, it was my turn. I wanted to beat my brother and give my dad a run for his money. And seemingly with little effort, I imitated the sound correctly, just like that! I could catch onto things quickly, and the belching game was only one example.

"Wow, Fatty." I not only surprised myself but also my dad and siblings.

I was the winner of the Bostic belching contest!

"First place! Big mama wins!" my dad announced, cheering and giving me a high-five at the same time.

"What's the prize for winning first place?" I excitedly asked.

"McDonald's," he announced.

I loved me some McDonald's, especially their French fries.

"Aww, man," my siblings whined.

There was another side to my dad. When it came to our sports performances, he demanded perfection. It was about pushing past the limits and being the best we could possibly be. He was filled with a burning desire to see my brother make it to the NFL and my twin and I to the Olympics, winning the gold in track and field.

My older brother, Carlitos, was a talented musician. He played the drums. He was also great at running the football better than anyone in the neighborhood, even little league, like my dad. The coaches told him and my mom they had never seen anyone as gifted as Carlitos and he would go far in the game. He was the star of the family—Dog #99.

When it came to my sister and me, we were both athletic, dominating all events, and we loved field day, from the 100-yard dash to the shoe kick. I was first, she was second, or I was second, and she was first. We used the "tag-team" approach, and to me, there were no losers because we both were the top two. One summer, we even qualified for the Junior Olympics, straight out of the blocks, no training, as we'd race the 100-yard dash against all boys.

"Bet my girls can leave your boys in the dust," my dad boasted to the coach as we approached the track.

The coach laughed. "Man, get out of here. I've got the fastest boys in the race."

It was us against them. I really hated how my dad put us on the spot like that, but we had to perform and make him proud.

"On your mark, get set, go!" yelled the track coach.

I can still see my dad screaming like a crazy fan for us to run faster and push harder. First and second place. Bernadette and I were so excited, jumping up and down and hugging each other for our victory. We'd done it. We'd done it!

We left them in the dust to the point of disbelief as they walked off the track whining like a bunch of five-year-old's, dropping into a defeated huddle, sharing dry team support to those who were runners up.

They did their best to avoid us, but they had no choice but to congratulate us on our win. "It's you and me, sister," I said, hugging Bernadette as we walked off the track.

"Wonder twin power activated!"

"You have some gifted daughters; I've never seen girls run without the blocks." The coach excitedly approached my dad as we were walking off the field. "I'd like to invite them to be a part of our team and run with us in the Junior Olympics," he said. "I'm amazed by their talent and speed!" The speed on the track was one of our advantages.

Dad grinned. "Man, thank you; they get it from me."

Many years later, I asked my dad where he got his passion and drive from. He paused. He had grown children who had far surpassed any expectations he could have dreamed of for them, let alone himself. At this point, he was older, wiser, and more selfless.

"In my life, when chasing my dreams, I have seen what the world can do to people, but women seem to have the power to manipulate. A woman with a pretty face and curves can run the world. I have done some things that I pray every day God forgives me for," he told me. "I just wanted to make sure my kids had the best opportunities in life. See, you and your sister are so pretty, like Muhammad Ali's twins. I see them, and I see you guys. You guys are the greatest, and to get anything in life, you, your sister, and brothers have to work hard to get it."

As a father, he was loving, full of fun, and devoted. He encouraged us to be the best—whether it was belching or playing sports—and to dream and always be dressed, even if we were just going to the store. Above all, we were taught to keep God first.

My mom wasn't pleased with our dad teaching us how to belch, and she didn't go to church. "That's not for girls or teaching them good manners," she'd always cry. But the thing is we didn't belch in public places, just in the comfort of our home.

Mom was beautiful, tall, and slender, with large breasts and long legs complemented by her butter-colored complexion. She wore her fiery red hair in an Afro, and she had blazing brown eyes. She was the Foxy Brown of our family. She was a hint of black and proud trapped in a white woman's skin.

My mom was the queen of makeup, from the blue eyeshadows, rose blushes, lipsticks, and glosses. My mother could go from casual to business to jazzy and sexy; her nightgowns were gorgeous, like ballroom dresses. Her rings and earrings ranged from gold to silver. She had diamond rings, necklaces, and bangles of all colors. Her jewelry box resembled discovered sunken treasure.

On Thanksgiving, I loved the peppermint candy baskets filled with nuts and fruit specially delivered from the Thornhill family, who owned the largest peppermint factory in Pittsburgh, Pennsylvania.

My mother shared some of her childhood stories about being raised by her grandmother. "My parents divorced when I was two years old."

"Wow, you were just a baby."

"Yeah." She sighed. "Then my mother and father disappeared—

just vanished. Your Aunt Jackie and I became wards of the state, and we stayed with my grandmother, who worked as a maid for the rich white college professors in Ann Arbor.

"I was an angry little girl, hated my parents, thankful for my grandmother raising us. But she always called me Dumb Dora, said, 'You are going to end up like your mother,'" she continued to share. "My mom was an alcoholic and lived life her way. Meanwhile, my sister was always sassy, cute, and could get away with anything.

"Then, at fifteen, I met your dad." She smiled as her eyes sparkled. "Got pregnant, married at sixteen; four years later, I had twins—you and Bernadette."

My mother was my hero. Despite those odds, she was beautiful and smart. I can remember my mother working days and going to college at night to get her education and a better occupation for herself and her children. So I can see why she was the backbone, the educator of our family and why her children's academic success was significant to her. If my brother, sister, and I didn't bring home A's and B's, we were in big trouble. Speaking proper English, reading, and writing were crucial, and Hooked on Phonics was our Bible.

Every Friday was Fun Night during my early childhood, from memorable meals to board games. My mother was off work, and it was family game night. She'd cook her famous cheeseburgers and home-cooked French fries made from huge Idaho potatoes. And for dessert, she would make popcorn and chocolate malts while we played Life, Monopoly, Scrabble, Connect Four, Family Feud, or You Sank My Battleship. Board games were our childhood entertainment. Saturday mornings were the best. We had Pancake Saturday—pancakes with chocolate chips and bacon on the side.

Everything was perfect, but my fairytale family would soon become a nightmare on Hamilton Street.

3

IT'S A TWIN THING

I heard that when God creates a face he really likes, he creates twins. So I guess he really liked me because, yes, I am an identical mirror twin to Bernadette, who's older than me by only six minutes. I believed God wanted to show my mother how much he loved her by giving her a unique phenomenon—identical mirror twins.

Identical Mirror Twin? You might be asking yourself. The term "identical mirror" describes a characteristic where some identical twins' features appear asymmetrically—that is, on opposite sides. It's a unique visual effect in such that when they are facing each other, the twins seem to be reflections, as if looking in a mirror. For example, my sister is left-handed, and I'm right. Our cowlicks—hers runs clockwise, and mine counterclockwise. Our voices, gestures, and movements mirror each other too, like when we wave simultaneously, her with the right hand and me with the left. Scientific research says that the one dominant on the left side of the brain may be more assertive in skills that require logic or analysis rather than intuition or creativity. I think they got that one wrong because we share all four of those qualities at different times, or all at the same time when we are together or apart, even today. We still finish each other's sentences. It's like we have a secret gift to see things and read minds, not just of ourselves, but for others too.

Our identicalness was a blessing and a curse at times, which was frustrating. As identical mirror twins, it was hard not to notice how fascinated the rest of the world was by our sibling relationship. We spent much of our time answering annoying questions, from "Who's the oldest?" to, "How can I tell you two apart?" Even "How does it feel to be a twin?" Oh, and this famous one: "Can you feel what she feels or know what she's thinking?"

Where did people get the idea that being a twin was the perfect sibling relationship? That really is a myth. In our early childhood, we dressed alike, from our clothes to hairstyles. We were modeled in local fashion shows. My mom even entered us into a twin contest—but we lost because, while we are identical, our outfits were different colors.

And how can I forget hearing those comments that created a sense of competition between us, like, "Who's the prettiest?" or "Who's the mean one?" I loved the attention, but Bernadette hated it.

"Hey, Antoinette," someone would yell to my sister.

"I'm not her," she'd shriek in response. There were countless moments of mistaken identity, when someone else mistook me for my sister or the other way around. I felt she didn't want anyone to compare us in our similarities but notice her differences. That was like looking for a needle in a haystack. Keeping that closeness and harmony between us was challenging for us both.

We had the usual rivalry and spats between sisters. Between the two of us were broken toys, destruction of violin bows and saxophone reeds, torn clothes, and scratches and blows.

We fought to be different.

Big brother Carlitos was four years older than Bernadette and me. He was always involved in sports leagues and band, so that kept him away from home a lot, but for some strange reason, when he was home, the two would always tag team me, teasing me about my gapped front teeth, mimicking me and calling me Marlene Jr. They were bullies. At sixteen years old, he moved in with his high school football coach to play the sport. I was glad to see him go and sad that I was stuck at home. Boy, did he have luck.

As a twin, I savored attention. I also began to feel the pressure and frustration that came with us always being tied and compared to each other. Hats off to Dad, who set the bar for an intense competition between my sister and me. It also made it difficult for us to forge our separate identities. It was a fierce competition as we struggled to develop our own identities beyond one half of a duo.

Bernadette was the gracious twin, always rescuing stray cats and dogs, bringing them home, feeding them Dad's favorite dessert—cheesecake—or sneaking Oreo cookies and snacks to the neighborhood kids. She loved to dress up in fairytale costumes like Snow White, and playing with her collection of hundreds of Barbie dolls was her addiction. She was also the artist, always drawing eyes and entering contests, seeing who could draw the best characters, a pirate or a person, with a grand prize of five thousand dollars, which she never won.

I was the tomboy, less emotional, and my imaginations of being the police were real, from dressing up on Halloween, wearing my badge and shiny black hat, to carrying fake gray plastic handcuffs, keys, and radio. I had all types of toy guns, from the cap gun—a

23

silver revolver with five red paper rolls of caps that loudly went *POP!*
POP! like a gunshot with a puff of smoke—to the air rifle and B.B.
gun. I had a pretty good idea of what I wanted to be. I played with
Crime Scene Investigations Real Life Science Activities to learn
about collecting evidence, dusting for fingerprints, lifting fingerprints, and examining blood splatter.

I had a crazy infatuation for bugs. You name it, I trapped them,
fed them, freeze-dried them, and used mothballs to study them. I
wanted to find out how creatures lived and killed, so I studied ant
and worm farms and housed spiders in jars and roaches in glue
boxes. I persuaded my mother to purchase me doctor kits, science
and chemistry kits with microscopes, dyes, and slides, and even
the Creepy Crawlers Bug Maker, which allowed me to make bugs
that felt like slime. My little corner in the basement was my own
science lab.

I would collect water from rain puddles covered in moldy leaves,
producing funky odors of plant decay. No sooner had I touched one
drop of pond water to a glass slide under the microscope than a world
leaped to life. Hundreds of bacteria crowded into view, resembling
rush hour traffic. *It's alive!* My curiosity would provide me with a
sense of confidence. As a student at George Elementary School, I
won the first-place ribbons and prizes in science fairs from fourth
grade through sixth grade.

My dad was excited about his athletically gifted son and boastful
and proud of his identical twin girls, our cuteness and speed on the
track, while Mom was stern on academic achievements and cleanliness. "Cleanliness is next to godliness" was her favorite line that
she got from her grandmother. My parents raised us according to
their strengths: my brother, twin sister, and I were directed by their
combined energies and good parenting, which shaped us.

Those were the days.

This is where living in a small town became my worst undoing. Everyone knew the good, the bad, and the ugly or pretended as if nothing was happening because they turned a blind eye. At a young age, I was dealt misfortunes in life like sickness and disease that took over the lives of those I loved. We saw families in the community lose clothes, furniture, and photo albums filled with memories due to house fires. Their needs were significant, and we lost friends and family who died unexpectedly in car accidents or by sudden death. I was a witness to some hard times.

As a kid, I learned more from people watching than overhearing adult conversations during family gatherings or by sitting at the table during church dinners as saints chattered about the menu to members. And from the visits to Aunt Jackie's, when they would have girlfriends over, airing dirty laundry. But I also learned from what I saw. I paid attention to the details of non-verbal and verbal communication wherever I was and whoever it was.

Let me paint you a few pictures of what I mean before labeling me a psychic or abnormal. With my dad working afternoons and my mother using all three shifts—swinging between midnights, days, and afternoons too—Mom was forced to hire Sam, short for Samantha, as our new babysitter. Our lives were like ships passing in the night. I would see my dad and mom for brief moments between their jobs, and my siblings and I would spend more time with Sam than our parents.

Then the arguments began. My mom wasn't happy about my dad's lifestyle. "How many times have I told you I don't want your friends and their girlfriends over when I'm not home!" my mother yelled. "The smoking and the drinking ... I have to clean up beer cans and cigarette butts when I get off work."

"The kids are in bed when they come over!" he would holler. "You're never home anyway."

"Never home?" she cried. "I'm working twelve-hour shifts to help pay the bills and make some extra money to get my hair done." The yelling continued, and then I could hear thumping and rumbling around. My parents were fighting. They were always fighting. They were no longer like Ashford & Simpson, "Solid as a rock." They became like Ike and Tina Turner—very abusive. *What's love got to do with it?* I'd ask myself. Sometimes I wondered if my parents even knew we existed.

After the yelling and fighting stopped, I'd lay still in bed, clutching my covers, crying silently as tears rolled down my face. I watched my father invest himself more and more into his desires and goals instead of being a dad to me, Bernadette, and Carlitos, let alone being a husband to my mother. He drifted away. What could be more important to my father that he'd forget about us?

My parents divorced, and unexpectantly, my dad left to follow his dreams of being an actor. He moved to Hollywood. I was devasted, questioning, *Does a parent have to let go of their family to follow their dreams?* I wanted the attention and love that was once there.

It didn't take a rocket scientist to know that my parents hadn't been happily married. In fact, the sheer volume of arguments, fights, name calling, and looks of disgust at each other were very telling that they clearly weren't going to make it. When I think back, I didn't just see signs of what was truly going on; the evidence was staring us all in the face. But when you don't want to confront something, the safest thing to do to protect your feelings and your ego is to ignore it and pray it gets better. And that's what I think we all did, at least for a while.

* * *

Having parents in two different states meant traveling during holidays and vacations. One summer, two years later, when I was nine years old, Carlitos, Bernadette, and I flew to Hollywood to see my dad. The front door of my dad's apartment opened as we walked up the sidewalk, and there she was, standing and grinning as if she was happy to see us.

I felt myself drift back in time, to when I was seven years old and saw her coming to open the front door of my house. The cut-off shirt, the Daisy Dukes, soup-cooler lips, Farah Fawcett hair—it was the babysitter, the wicked witch of the west. My stomach flipped, and I dropped my bags.

"Jesus," I whispered, pulling back a step, almost falling to my knees. I hadn't even realized I'd said it out loud. "What is she doing here?" My sister and brother probably had the same reaction, but they kept it to themselves. But my dad caught my expression and the words that matched my response. The cat was finally out of the bag.

"Everything is okay" was the response he used to so-called calm me down.

Dazedly, shaking my head in disbelief, I thought to myself, *Ain't this about a bitch!*

"What do you mean she stays here?" I asked my dad. I needed some answers and needed them quick.

"Aww, Fatty, don't be like that," he pleaded as he tried to use those, "I'll bite your neck" silly routines. But there was nothing funny.

"So, you two live together?" I screamed, not just for me, but for my mother. I became angry at him for so many reasons, for lying about following his dream, sleeping with the babysitter while he was married to my mom, then the two of them running away together. We didn't even matter. And just think, I blamed my mother for his disappearance.

That summer vacation was a trip to hell, and it changed me; the anger and confusion overwhelmed me, and inwardly, I shut down emotionally, trying to figure out how and why my dad would be with the babysitter instead of me … us.

★   ★   ★

Fast forward. It was Friday night, and I walked that long road to the altar. It's burned into my mind. I was ten years old. We were seated in the second-to-last row of the Messiahs Temple Apostolic Church with my Aunt Jackie when the guest speaker began. It was as if he was talking directly to me: "Jesus bottles up every tear; he died so we could live, and God loves you. There isn't anyone he loves more than you." He stepped off the pulpit and made an altar call for anyone who wanted to be saved.

How did he know I cried myself to sleep most nights and that I didn't care about life anymore? I was baptized in Jesus' name, filled with the Holy Spirit, with the evidence of speaking in another language. After it was all over, people came up and congratulated me. I felt lighter than I'd ever felt; I was floating on air. I wrote it as my newfound salvation. That feeling lasted about a week. In my church back home, you were never really saved, not for good. The church was very strict, so one could always lose their salvation by their attire, makeup, jewelry, watching television, celebrating Christmas or Easter—these were things the church considered worldly—something that could cause one to miss the Rapture. To top it off, there were my mother's rollercoaster dating relationships.

Then she suddenly got married again without sharing it with any of us. It came without warning, a total shock to Carlitos, Bernadette, and me. Our dad's calls were inconsistent; we felt that he wasn't sincere, and when the needs stopped, it was apparent that he wasn't honest from the onset. His promises of birthday gifts and Christmas presents never came.

I was disappointed and angry that he didn't keep his word. How could he do that to us? How could he do that to me? It became personal. Then out of nowhere, my mom got married to this guy who she'd only known for three weeks, and they joined the church too. They made sure we were at church every time the doors opened, which happened to be twice on Sunday, Tuesday for young people, Wednesday for Bible class, Thursday for missionary, and Friday evening for praise service. Five days out of the week; it was our second home.

School kids labeled us as different and strange. We were bullied for how we dressed, our hair style, and our eye color. I had a hard time fitting in. I missed my dad and hated being teased because of how I dressed—skirts, short socks, and gym shoes—and the comments about my hazel eyes and curly hair. Let's not forget I was flat as a board, with no breasts, no butt, and I was called "white girl" by others. My mind soaked up all such messages, and they fueled my constant fear of what I looked like and what might keep me out of heaven.

Church encouraged us to repent for sins we might not be aware of, just in case we forgot something. Over and over, I cried out to God for forgiveness because I felt he was punishing me. In my tween and early teens, I began to question if God loved me and thought of him as a scorekeeper. Whether it was the pastor's sermons, Sunday school lessons, the week-long revivals, or the yearly viewing of those awful movies, my church experience would become one soaked in anxiety. *Did I forget to repent of some sin? How long has it been since I've spoken in tongues? Am I living godly enough?* Tough questions for a kid.

I fought a lot and rebelled, not knowing how to deal with my frustration. I was angry at the world and my dad for leaving us. There were times I even took up for my sister. In fifth grade, after school while riding the bus, I was sitting in the back while my twin was seated closer to the front. I heard this girl Sonja sitting behind her, making jokes about my mother, and no one joked about my mother. That was against the rules for sure!

"Sonja, don't talk about our mother," I yelled, running to rescue my sister.

"What are you going to do?" she replied.

The other kids on the bus were going wild, expecting a fight. Making sure my sister was okay, I didn't respond.

"Meet me off the bus, and I'm going to kick your ass," Sonja huffed. When the bus came to a halt at our stop, it was on. What happened next was like a bout between Mike Tyson and Floyd Mayweather. A crowd swelled around us, and Sonja slapped me in my face. I clutched my lunchbox and aimed for her head, but she ducked, and she ran for her house. I chased her down, taking my lunchbox, and this time, I didn't miss. *Wham!* She fell to the ground, and I ran home, only to have my mother walk me back to Sonja's and apologize. How unfair.

"Do as I say do, not as you see me do" or "Children are to be seen and not heard" were the anthems of adults, which caused me to pay less attention to their words and more to their actions, be it verbal or non-verbal communication. I saw adults contradict the lifestyle that was taught across the pulpit.

For many years, and in so many ways, church and religion became more of a cult in my life. It was all about helping others or dressing in dictated attire. I saw how adults had double standards and how they committed sins. Good things became "God things," and it often kept me from being close to my family.

Growing up in church played a significant part in my life as a child. It helped me develop some perspectives, beliefs, and understandings. Many of these beliefs I grew up with, I now consider half-truths or outrightly false. However, some of these beliefs were quite weird and humorous at the same time. If you grew up in a staunch religious culture, you might be able to relate. Then again, you may not. You may even be offended by these beliefs, knowing what they genuinely are or represent.

Regardless, I want to make this quite clear—these perspectives, beliefs, and understandings were solely the products of my teenage mind, based on observations and verbal and non-verbal communication. Just as I said, they were the products of an inquisitive young girl, who may have been gifted with a keen sixth sense of sight.

I had grown accustomed to attending church religiously. This was the norm, and I could finish the pastor's scriptures during his message because I read the Bible like it was a comic book. But over time, my awareness of stark differences between the church I attended with my family vs. others that we visited began to affect my ability to focus because so many rules set by the church took the joy out of being a kid. The differences were too significant to ignore, from how the church was conducted to even how they dressed; it seemed that the religious folks were mostly concerned about putting up an appearance and not being holy like they would have us believe.

Struggling with understanding and my observation, I rebelled against my mother and the church's holy standards with gusto. I tried to live as far away from the rules as possible, from wearing pants, listening to R&B, wearing makeup, and playing cards. I even kissed boys—the ones who wanted to, and that wasn't many. I grew increasingly bitter, angry, and repulsed by anything related to the church. The life of double standards—the lies and betrayals coming from people in the church, whom I trusted and respected—created chaos, and I was drowning is confusion, praying that God would help me sort all of this confusion that was invading my space.

My mom knew I had a fascination with police when I was as young as twelve years old. So, she allowed me to stay up past my bedtime to see the premiere of *Hill Street Blues*, a police drama that showcased the struggles that cops encountered in the workplace and their personal lives, between doing "what is right" and "what works." I loved women in police dramas. Watching police dramas and reading crime stories, I pictured myself in each one of them. Investigating crime scenes and searching for clues led me to discover who did it before the show's end. I would escape the noise around me by diving into books like *Nancy Drew* and *The Hardy Boys*, or even by reading the Bible and discovering people in the Bible had just as much drama or more as my parents and the church did. I was faithful to my crime and mystery dramas.

I loved reading the newspaper so much that I asked my mom if I could be the papergirl, to deliver the *Ypsilanti Press* just to read my favorite sections—the obituaries and crime blotters—and get paid. On Sunday mornings, upon discovering that the *Detroit News* and *Detroit Free Press* would be part of my delivery, I was always fascinated because I knew I would be rewarded with expositions to the stories of crime and death in the big city!

One Sunday morning, I picked up the *Ypsilanti Free Press*, our local newspaper, and was drawn to the obituaries and the crime blotter, curious to see who died and what crimes were committed. I imagined I was a detective investigating the deaths, trying to solve the crimes, catch the criminals, and close the cases. No fears, only intrigue.

CHAPTER

4

WHAT HAPPENS IN VEGAS

At age fifteen, I was an all-A student who had a college-prep curriculum. I had worked hard for those grades, and my love for police crime drama grew into an addiction, and it showed. I watched *Cagney and Lacey, T.J. Hooker, Policewoman, C.H.I.P.S.,* and *X-Files*. Each was inspirational for me, showing me that I could become anything, especially a cop, a for-men-only job.

The shows revealed women's personal struggles and their successes behind the badge and their intimate relationships—be it in marriage, parenting, or dating—which were complicated to some extent. The shows were thought provoking, entertaining, and they glamorized the profession. Being a cop or detective was portrayed as an occupation that women could aspire to. It inspired little girls to think outside of being a housewife, princess, or queen. Becoming a cop was real for me. Time and circumstances proved that it was my destiny.

That summer, I really missed my father, and I wondered if he missed me too. It had been years since I had seen him and months since we talked. I wanted to share my dreams with him and get his approval. I asked Mom if I could visit him for my summer vacation. She agreed. Then I made the phone call, putting his past failures behind, keeping my fingers crossed, and prayed that he still loved me enough to want to see me so I could get away.

"Dad, I miss you. Can I come visit for the summer?" I asked, my heart pounding between words.

"Sure, Fatty, you can come. I'll buy the ticket today."

And so he did. I spent my entire summer with him—June, July, and August—all by myself. In the days leading up to my trip, I attempted to put together the perfect outfits, but unfortunately, all my closets and drawers contained long skirts, long dresses, t-shirts, and socks.

The hour had finally arrived; it was time to head to the Detroit Metropolitan Airport to fly out to see my dad.

"You really going to Daddy's?" Bernadette asked as we jumped into the car's back seat while my mom and her husband, Jack, put my luggage in the trunk.

"Bern, yes," I said with a half-smile. Deep inside, I really wasn't sure, but what I was sure of was that I had to make a getaway!

"You know how Daddy is. He cheated on Mama with the babysitter, and he hasn't kept any of his promises to us!" she said, staring me straight in the face.

I sat back, looking out the window. Past the half-built subdivision and empty cement lots, I could see a row of airplanes coming in and others lifting off into the sunset. We were getting close. In a few hours, my plane would be taxiing onto the runway. I began to question myself: Did I really want to go to my dad's?

Yes. And no.

I knew Dad cheated on Mom with the babysitter and God only

knows with who else. I knew he broke his promises, like forgetting to send our Christmas and birthday gifts when he said they were in the mail and on the way. Yes, my dad was a liar. But he had kept his word this time; he bought my ticket when I asked, and that was all that mattered to me. I loved him anyway, and perhaps he'd changed.

A skinny, blossoming teen with braces, I was off to Las Vegas all by myself.

"It's a sunny and clear afternoon, ladies and gentlemen. A beautiful day in Las Vegas, ninety-five degrees on the ground. A light breeze from the southwest. Sit back and relax; we'll be landing shortly."

The wheels roared out of the bottom of the plane, and it began to descend. I could see Las Vegas; it was surrounded by mountains, deserts, green palm trees, and grass in certain places. Every house and casino was dotted with blue swimming pools. I was excited to be seeing my dad, yet my mind was on being back home.

I arrived at my dad's house. He disapproved of my attire. It wasn't my fault that my mother dressed my sister and me in clothes that made us appear like we were in *Little House on the Prairie*. But my dad wasn't having it.

"Why does your mother have you dressed like you're Amish?" he roared. "Your hair is in ponytails and barrettes. You have bushy eyebrows; your blouse is up to your neck, and your skirt is to the floor. White socks and white gym shoes—you look like you just walked off the farm." From the time we picked up my luggage until we got to his car, he cussed, fussed, and questioned my mama about my looks.

"Hey, don't talk about my Chuck Taylor All-Stars. I love my gym shoes!"

My dad had my hair cut and styled within hours of my plane landing. My eyebrows were shaved pencil thin, and my face was painted dark and gothic, with heavy black eyeshadow, liner, mascara, and red lipstick. Then off to the mall. He picked out all the outfits, having me try on each one to see how it fit.

"My mom would kill me and you if she saw me dressed like this!" I yelled, slamming the door. I felt like I was on a runway, modeling in a fashion show. I looked at the mirror but saw a different girl. She looked just like me but older. Was this real, or was I really seeing things in the three-way-mirrored dressing room? *Maybe it's the heat or the jetlag,* I thought, trying to convince myself. *Vegas, ninety-five degrees; my flight was long, and I'm now three hours behind Michigan time, so I've been up for hours, not minutes.*

"Is it Halloween?" I looked like a combination of Madonna and Vanity 6. Turning and twisting in the mirror, I asked myself, *Who is this girl?*

"Careful, Antoinette," a voice screamed.

"Wha—" I was a deer in headlights in the mirror; my reflection's eyes were wide, her mouth open like a warning; then she was overshadowed by a dark figure. When I turned, my dad opened the dressing room door.

"There's my fox," he said as he admired me in the dark brown buttoned pinstriped suit he'd picked out. "I love those heels and stockings; better than the gym shoes and white socks your mama had you dressed in. Keep that on. You're coming with me." I thought he was concerned about my being alone, but it was more than that.

We went to the Penthouse Casino, where my dad was the events manager for the Miss Black America beauty contest, the main attraction. Beyond the lights, the slots, and poker tables, behind the stage, I would be introduced to a tribe of beautiful brown girls, all shades of color, midnight black to red dirt, and canary yellow. They were all packaged differently, but tall and slim were the typical characters.

"Fox, you see all these pretty girls?"

"Yes, they are beautiful."

"Not only are they pretty, but they're also smart, educated, and know how to hustle," he said as he pointed to every girl that passed by. "And that's how I see you!" he said, smiling.

From that moment on, my dad introduced grown men to me. He shared that they were wealthy; some were part of the casino empire; others owned construction companies or were part of the security and entertainment industry. Some were even pastors. These men weren't dressed in flashy suits, accented with large chains and diamonds; they were casually dressed in slacks, button-down Polos with blazers, Rolex watches, and simple yet elegant rings worn on various fingers. Some were married. I knew the wedding finger.

The men varied in color, shapes, and age. Some were black, biracial, or white, fat, skinny, baby faced, clean shaven, or bald with gray beards.

Many complimented my dad for having such a beautiful daughter.

"Yeah, I got a fox, and she's an identical twin," was his response. I felt like I was being showcased like a classic car at an auction.

Then the most bizarre thing happened. One of the men, who was older and graying but handsome, and who my father introduced as Mr. Rich, approached us later, asking Dad if he could take me out for dinner.

"Sure, man," my dad said with a stutter, grinning.

"Dad, I'm just fifteen years old," I whispered, smiling and gritting my teeth. I was too young to even buy a drink, let alone go out to dinner with a grown man by myself.

"The man is just being nice and trying to show you a good time." He looked me in the eyes. "Now you go and enjoy yourself. You're in good hands, and I'll see you later." He pushed me to go instead of protecting me by making me stay.

I wasn't comfortable with going out to dinner with a man who was old enough to be my father, but I trusted my dad and, more than anything, I wanted his approval.

"After you, my princess," Mr. Rich said as he escorted me to the elevator.

"Thank you, Mr. Rich." I smiled and waved goodbye to my dad as the doors closed.

"Call me, Sam." He handed the valet his parking ticket. "You're a beautiful girl, and I love your eyes." The valet arrived with his silver Bentley. The silence in the car was eerie; I could hear and feel my heart beating in my throat. After a journey that took almost thirty minutes, we finally arrived at Sam's house. I had never seen, much less been inside, houses that big. This guy was wealthy. His home was nestled in a gated community somewhere in Las Vegas; it was dark, and the mountains looked like blue clouds against the sky.

As we rode past a beautiful swimming pool, green grass, and palm trees, dimmed lights guided us to a tall black door that opened into a den, and led us through the kitchen and to the living room. I had never been alone with a man, let alone with a man in a mansion. I was fascinated.

"Get comfortable," he ordered while taking off his shoes and tie, throwing them on the couch, "Take your shoes off. Would you like anything to drink?" he said, walking into the kitchen and unbuttoning his shirt.

"I'll have whatever you're having," I said, a line I remembered from one of my police shows. I'd never tasted alcohol before. As I sipped on the drink, thinking it was iced tea, behold, I learned it was an alcoholic beverage.

Sam began to rub my feet, moving up my legs. He began pulling my stockings off when he asked me to lie on my stomach. I was scared … terrified. I closed my eyes, and all I could hear was my dad saying, "This is a nice man. Enjoy yourself." As Sam continued to rub on me, now at my thighs, he asked me questions about my family, life, grades, boyfriends, favorite desserts, what I wanted to be, and where I wanted to live when I grew up.

He was listening. Sam shared he came from humble beginnings as a construction owner. His wealth as an entrepreneur in the construction business opened opportunities for contracts of multiple projects, including building in Las Vegas and Atlantic City, from casinos to stadiums, arenas, and churches across the country. He gained a circle of friends in influential positions within the criminal justice system, government, and the church.

"If you ever decide to stay here in Las Vegas, I'll help you to be whatever you want."

What an offer, I thought to myself. I was with a total stranger who might get me somewhere in life. He asked me more personal questions than my parents, and he didn't preach about dress codes and sin.

"Turn over now," Sam requested as he finished rubbing my back. When I did, he was totally naked, gray-haired, freckled chest and all. I didn't know what to do. I froze. Sam told me there was nothing to be afraid of and I was safe. He promised I wouldn't have to do anything I didn't want to.

I believed him and guessed that this was what men with money and position did. I guessed my dad was right—I was in good hands. He kissed my neck, and I could feel a tingling sensation all through my body as his tongue slid down to my breast. I was hot all over. Sam licked his fingers and began playing with my vagina. I felt flushed.

He caressed me all over. I was slowly building up to his fondling when I felt this fire between my legs. Suddenly, he was thrusting his big penis inside of me and panting heavily.

"Get off me!" I kicked, screamed, and cried. I had never felt pain like that.

"Why are you crying like a little girl?"

"Because I am. I'm only fifteen years old!" I sobbed.

"Fifteen years old?!" he exclaimed. "Get dressed so I can take you back to your daddy." He hopped up and threw my clothes and three hundred dollars at me. How he knew where my father lived baffled me. I was in shock. But it didn't stop there.

Date after date, my dad would allow men he knew that were his age and older to visit and take me out for "ice cream."

What father would do that? I asked myself. I was confused and sick to my stomach. I wondered if he knew what he was doing and the impact it was having on me; it confused me, and I didn't always know how to respond.

My dad still found ways to reassure me and diminish my concerns, sometimes teasingly dismissing my discomfort by using his favorite line: "Go ahead; he's trying to be nice." And I began to believe that if there were any problems with the situation, they were mine—my way of thinking, my more old-fashioned church upbringing.

Nevertheless, I gained a sense of confidence, control, and cleverness. I wasn't the same scared girl on that first, second, or third date. I would be chauffeured in a limo to more gated communities of mansions that were hidden in the mountains or beyond the palm trees, far from the Las Vegas Strip.

"Did you have a good time?" my dad asked whenever I returned.

Did I have a good time? I couldn't believe that was his only question for me.

On one date—I am not sure of the number, because there were so many, but it was on the Fourth of July; I remember the fireworks—my dad introduced me to Derrick, whose father was head of a central basketball team. It was love at first sight. Derrick was not old like the others; he was tall and lean, kind of on the street side, mixed with a little white boy thrown in.

This time, I was excited and glad to go because the guy in question was fresh and good looking, with blonde hair, golden-tan smooth skin, not wrinkly like my other dates, and he smelled like a breath of fresh air. Derrick was twenty-two years old, and he was mixed—his mother was German, and his dad was Cherokee. He was fine!

"You're in good hands. I'll see you later." It was the typical parting words my father would utter. My dad's sendoff was now routine.

"You want to ride to L.A.?" Derrick said as we walked out the door and hopped in his convertible red two-seater.

"Sure!" I was excited, and I was getting away from Las Vegas.

From L. A. to the Sunset Strip, we partied at the clubs, drank champagne that tasted like Sprite, only dark and sweeter—Moet Imperial Nectar was the name—then we stopped by Venice Beach. It was like a scene out of the movies. The roaring blue waters crashed on the warm sand and ran through my toes as the swaying palm trees danced in the breeze. I was in heaven and didn't want to leave. For the first time since being at my dad's, I had fun, and it had nothing to do with sex.

No more dates for me. I was taken for the remaining summer. God had sent me an angel named Derrick. He picked me up early afternoon every day. I didn't care what we did, and when sex happened, I felt like I never had before with the others. It was a feeling like when I watched *General Hospital* when Luke married Laura. It felt so right. The only time I saw my dad was to change clothes.

You'd think he'd be upset and put me on punishment, but he didn't. "You must really like him" was the only thing my dad said to me about Derrick.

"Yes, I do," I replied, leaving out the door to escape.

"The man is just being nice and trying to show you a good time" and "Go ahead; he's trying to be nice" were words I would never have to hear from my dad again.

I was encouraged to do sexual exploration by a person whom I trusted—my dad. This was very traumatic for me. I didn't know what or how to respond or if I should tell my mom, but I think it groomed me for what was to come. I let men touch me while I sat there disgusted and ashamed. They probed me, connected me with their perverted fingers and penises, licked my flesh, and sucked on my nipples with their disgusting mouths.

It was sin … a sin that I brought upon myself. The evil that I wouldn't need to bear if I didn't let it happen. How could something so filthy make my body tingle like electrical currents running from my toes to the tips of my fingers?

That summer, I learned lessons about men, power, and control. I sometimes felt guilty for allowing the sins of men and their insatiable lust to sentence me to a life of shame, filth, hurt, and anger that had taken me hostage. And to think, I'd probably never see myself again … at least not the innocent girl who had left home for a summer trip to Vegas.

CHAPTER
5
WELL GROOMED

September 1984. I returned home from my Las Vegas summer vacation a different girl. What happens in Vegas doesn't stay in Vegas; what happened to me that summer came home with me like extra baggage. Everything had changed, and I saw the world differently. I was no longer unaware of the darkness that was preached and talked about in church; I was now the girl exposed and exploited in a world that was chaotic, twisted, and extremely wicked—I'd had up-close encounters in the place known as Sin City.

The beginning of a new school year was when most girls thought about clothes, boys, and hanging out at the mall with their girlfriends. But for me, I really didn't care about school, no matter how I tried to focus. Things at home worsened. The arguing between my mom and her husband became constant; the words I heard them shout at each other were the same words that had been passed between her and my dad. My mother was so caught up in her own issues and struggles that she couldn't see something horrific had happened to her daughter. I was lost and in trouble.

I made a rule that my stepfather couldn't hug me, and I started talking back to my mother. In the morning, while eating Captain Crunch Berries, I arranged cereal boxes to block anyone from seeing me; plus, I enjoyed reading the backs of the boxes. At dinner, bottles of A-1, ketchup, sauce bottles, or the flower centerpiece blocked my view of anyone sitting at the table.

The struggle of being a twin became even more pronounced. I think we both internalized our dad and the babysitter's affair in very different ways, not to mention Mom and Dad's divorce and her remarrying. I'll have to write about that in another book.

Going to church five days a week, I developed a love/hate relationship with it. Church, to me, was an escape from home. While there, I got to see friends, and Jesus would be there, but the staunch rules would get the best of me. I saw church so much clearer—as a thing of power and control, and it was cliquish, instead of being full of real love and family. I witnessed person after person point their fingers at other members who didn't fit the description, those whose behavior didn't meet their standards, the ones with the short, tight-fitting skirts, red lipstick, and blonde hair, who played secular or blues music.

I questioned how the hypocritical adults lived—ushering on Sunday and smoking on Monday; singing in the choir and sleeping with the drummer yet married to the piano player; finding every excuse for their choices, not thinking of the children and the impact. I hated everyone, including myself.

The eyes are the windows to the soul; I could see what people didn't say. I was no longer that little girl who paid attention to the details of adult behavior, their body language, imitating their gestures, the way a woman swayed her hips, the touching of hands or tapping of the shoulder, flipping of her hair and batting her eyes, that sudden deep gaze. I could hear them so loudly, instructing me to stay silent and do what they said.

By this time, I learned that church was about a spiritual relationship with God, a person's soul, and not what a person wore or their position. But I was falling like a plane, spiraling out of the sky on fire, and the demons were winning. I felt no love from my mother or the world around me. I struggled with sleep disturbances, low self-esteem, guilt, shame, anxiety, and no place to go.

Age ain't nothing but a number—that's what Las Vegas taught me.

* * *

I was about ten when I first met JB. Thanksgiving dinner was in the air, the hypnotizing aromas of turkey, dressing, cranberry sauce, homemade rolls, sweet potato pies, and pound cake. I was in heaven. Dinner was at the White's for the holiday. They were Carlitos' friends, but Bernadette and I got to tag along. I was sitting at the dining room table, and there he was. JB was seventeen or eighteen.

"Is anyone sitting here?" JB asked. He was a handsome boy; his face and chin were chiseled like a finely carved Michelangelo sculpture. His nose was perfectly proportioned. His lips were full; his smile was the kind that ended in a sly little smirk at the corners, accenting the dimples in his cheeks, the whip cream and cherry on top that made me want to eat him up for dessert. His caramel color complemented his chocolate eyes almost perfectly.

"What kind of cologne are you wearing?" I girlishly asked.

"Grey Flannel," he said, smiling. His manicured nails glistened in the candlelight.

The question about his cologne sparked a semi-lengthy conversation. Oh, of course, we asked each other the preliminary questions, such as each other's ages, where we lived, upbringing, schools, etcetera, etcetera. And that's when I discovered he was also junior deacon for one of Detroit's largest churches.

When I look back, I developed a girlish crush on JB almost immediately. Like the other men in my life—including my father, to an extent—JB was protective of me, and I'm reminded of the incident where my mind about him was made up, even though I was just fifteen and he was twenty-two.

Bernadette and I tagged along with Carlitos and his girlfriend to a cookout hosted in a local park. While playing spin the bottle with the other teens, it became painfully apparent that none of the boys wanted to kiss me. They even went as far as to state that they feared the wire from my braces would cause their lips to get stuck. The words stung, but more importantly, my esteem sank to a new low. I quit the game and ran all the way back to the house.

"What's the matter, pretty little girl in the red dress," JB said, having walked up on me.

"No one wants to kiss me," I cried.

"I'll kiss you," he said, smiling. He pressed his lips against mine. The softness of them seemed to melt the hurt I was experiencing. At that moment, I made up my mind—age was just a number, as the experience in Las Vegas had taught me. I was going to be with JB.

I didn't stop. I wrote letters professing my love for him and made nightly phone calls, discussing everything and nothing, even though he was engaged to be married to a city girl from his church who was attending the University of Michigan Medical School with dreams of becoming a doctor.

That late September, we made plans to meet at the church and go out on a date, grab a bite to eat at Big Boys, and find a hotel to get our freak on. But I couldn't go out by myself because our mother had a rule: "Where one goes, the other does too!" It's a twin thing. Bernadette was in on the plan because JB's brother Bill was coming too. It was a no-brainer.

We were set to go; it was a double date.

"I'll ask Mom if we can go to church and tell her that Willie is picking us up," I said to Bernadette. The plan was in motion. Following church, we went out to eat, and he pulled up to the Lamp Post Motel in Ann Arbor, far enough away so no one would recognize us.

"I'll be right back. Let me check and see if there's a vacancy," JB said as he parked and exited the car. While checking on the room, my twin, Bill, and I talked about if what we were doing was right.

"Maybe you should wait," Bernadette pleaded. But it was too late. By then, JB had come back to the car, swinging a set of keys.

"I got us a room, room sixty-four," he said as he shook the key in his hand and rolled around to the room.

Could this be fate? I asked myself. The number sixty-four represented my birthday, the sixth month, and the fourth day.

As we exited the car, Bernadette and JB's brother stayed behind. I was anxious, but I was also flattered that JB was even interested in me, even though I felt self-conscious since the Las Vegas experience. I showcased acne scars, braces, and a high school girlish look. I had nothing on his fiancée, who was away at medical school. Anyway, one thing led to another.

"Do you have a condom for protection?" I whispered.

"No, we don't need one. I'll pull out; I promise," JB reassured me and continued to slobber and suck on my neck. "That's what me and my girl use, and she hasn't gotten pregnant," he said, offering what I later discovered was a fake sense of assurance.

It was nothing like the Vegas escapades. It was over in a matter of seconds. He had ejaculated, and I was left wondering, *Is that all?* What was supposed to be a memorable moment turned out to be a flop.

CHAPTER

6

TEEN CONFESSION

My mom and I are weren't very close, so in the following weeks, when I began to feel sick, vomiting all throughout the day, she believed I had caught a stomach bug or the flu. But there was no fooling Bernadette. That's one thing about a twin; they know before they know. Only twins would understand this type of relationship.

"Ohhhh, you're pregnant," Bernadette whispered in my ear a time or two.

"No, I'm not. He used the pull-out method, so I'm protected," I responded with all manner of boldness. I couldn't have been more wrong. At that moment, reality hit me. I hated to think that my twin could be right. "Oh, my god! I don't know what I'm gonna do if I am pregnant! Mom is going to kill me." I wasn't sure at first what I was going to do. I mean, it wasn't like I could keep it a secret like I did about the rape in Vegas.

It wouldn't be too much longer before my mother would begin to question this mysterious, long-lasting flu.

* * *

"Antoinette, have you had your period?"

"Yes," I lied. *How does my mom know?*

"I haven't seen any pads in the bathroom garbage," she replied.

"I've been throwing the pads in my bedroom trashcan," I quickly answered.

Immediately, I started to throw away pads in the garbage to cover up what I expected—that I was pregnant.

"Let's call Aunt Jackie. She'll know how you should tell Mama about what happened and that you're pregnant," Bernadette suggested.

I couldn't keep it a secret. I was so scared I was pregnant. How could it be? I had sex all summer in Vegas without getting pregnant. But this time, my period was late. I was young and naïve and didn't think it could happen to me. JB and I had slept together only once.

"Aunt Jackie, can Bern and I come over? We have something to share and need your help to tell Mom." I just had this feeling, deep down within, that something was happening inside me.

"Sure, come on over," she replied. By the way, Aunt Jackie lived a hop, jump, and skip away from our house, literally, six blocks away.

"We're on our way." My twin and I tried to come up with a strategy for how to tell my aunt.

"Just tell her," my sister pleaded.

"Okay." My heart racing, Bernadette and I went to meet Aunt Jackie. There was no use in me trying to figure out a way to disguise my reason for wanting to meet with Aunt Jackie. I just came out with it.

"I think I'm pregnant," I tearfully confessed. I just cried my eyes out.

"Well, you know you have to tell your mother." Aunt Jackie was cool and calm.

"Are you serious?"

"Yes, you have to tell her. No secrets," Aunt Jackie said, persuading me. She took Bernadette and me back home, where I would have to do something I was not prepared to do … look my mother in the eye and tell her that her worst nightmare had come true—I was pregnant.

My mother opened the door to let us in. Somehow, I think she knew why we were all there. But Aunt Jackie made the preliminary announcement anyway.

"We need to talk to you. Antionette has something to tell you," Aunt Jackie said as we all shuffled into the living room. An eerie silence crept in. Aunt Jackie looked at me and nodded.

I drew a quick, deep breath and looked up, trying not to cry. I couldn't keep it a secret anymore, "I think I'm pregnant."

"You think you're *what*?" my mother questioned as if she wanted to make sure she didn't hear things.

"I … I think I'm pregnant," I repeated in a soft whisper.

"What? You think you're pregnant?!" yelled Mom, sharply looking at each of us. Her brown eyes were now flaming red.

"It's JB's? Right? Right!" she screamed.

How does she know?

"I know about you two." She began to cry. "I don't understand, Antionette. Why?"

I sat quietly. I watched as my mother ran her fingers through her hair, fumbled with her skirt, and then clasped her hands together. There was no doubt that she was utterly devastated.

The next day, it was off to Planned Parenthood to have a pregnancy test.

"It's positive; you're pregnant," the doctor said as he lowered his glasses, confirming my suspicion. My mom and I didn't look at each other; silence filled the space. I could tell my mother was disappointed and heartbroken more than she was mad. I think that was because she had my older brother when she was only sixteen and didn't want her daughters to experience being a teenage mother.

She cried almost every day. I grew tired of walking in on her outbursts because they made me feel even guiltier; needless to say, I felt ashamed and not worthy of her love. Of all the things I had done, I know that being pregnant topped them all, to the point that one day, she just came out with it.

"I want you to have an abortion."

"A what?"

"You heard me. I want you to have an abortion."

"Kill my baby?" I said, shocked and heartbroken at the same time. I couldn't believe that she, being a churchwoman, wanted me to do something so against the church's teachings. I already knew that, for me, having an abortion was out of the question.

"You're not in any position to take care of a baby."

"But Mom, I don't want to kill my baby," I defended.

"Who's going to take care of that baby? You don't think that boy is gonna stick around, do you?"

It was the first time I thought about the possibility of JB walking away. Let's face it, we pretty much had a secret relationship. No one, except our siblings, really knew that we saw each other.

"Do you?" my mother repeated.

"Well, it's still my child," I said, standing my ground, what little I had.

"I'm going to call the police and have him arrested for statutory rape."

"Mom, please don't do that! Please!" I begged. The dough was already in the oven, and I needed JB more than anything. I needed him by my side, not in jail. Tears began to stream down my cheeks.

"And I want to meet with his parents. He's a grown man, sleeping with a fifteen-year-old kid!" She let out a loud, piercing scream.

I heard what my mother was saying, but in my mind, I wasn't a kid. I had been introduced to grown-up things long ago. Although I'd had no intention of being a teenaged mother, I didn't have any doubts that I would be able to take care of my child.

My mom and Aunt Jackie put their heads together, and at some point, my mom called a meeting with JB and his parents at their home to discuss my being pregnant.

Days later, it was off to JB's parents' house, just me and my mother. The entire ride there was so quiet, you could hear a mouse piss on cotton. I'd heard that cliché many times, but I learned the true meaning that night.

When we arrived, Lydia, JB's mom, answered the door and greeted us. She and my mother were no strangers. My brother Carlitos dated Lydia's niece five years prior, and there was also a church affiliation causing them to be acquainted with each other. JB's father went to high school with my dad and knew some back history on our family.

"Yeah, I know your father," he boasted as we sat down to this long cherry-stained, elegant dining room table. The dining room was beautiful, and the peach carpet was so soft it was like walking on clouds.

JB entered the room, and we smiled at each other, trying to remain inconspicuous. It had been weeks since I had last seen him, and his caramel-brown skin, chiseled jaw, full lips, and brown eyes sparkled in the dining room light. The smell of his cologne would bring back the night when we were breast to breast. I was in love ... so I thought.

The conversation that night was turbulent. My mother cussed JB out for sleeping with her fifteen-year-old daughter.

"Don't you know you can go to jail?" she exclaimed. From their reaction, I could tell his parents had no idea JB was sleeping with an underage girl.

"JB, is that true?" his mother questioned. JB sat stiff, almost as though he had been caught off guard.

"What about your fiancée?" his mother commented.

"Did you know JB had life plans with someone else?" My mother's words echoed in my ears. I doubled over in tears. My mother, even in her anger and disappointment, began to rub my back.

JB's father seemed less interested in the fact that his son was cheating on his fiancée; he was more concerned about my age.

"Boy, what you are doing sleeping with a young girl ... when you're about to get married soon?!"

"I like Ann. She's a cute young lady, and I didn't plan on her getting pregnant," was JB's response.

JB's mother looked at me. "What do you want to be when you grow up?" The most common question adults ask children.

"I would like to be a homicide detective or mortician," I replied.

"Oh, wow, that's interesting. How are your grades?"

"I have a three-point-zero GPA in college prep courses." I was proud of my academic standing because, before this, my grade point average was 2.0.

Based on their silence, I guessed they were surprised that I wasn't some dumb teenager. I may have been pregnant, but I was smart in the books.

"This is how things are going to happen," my mother said. "JB, if you don't want to go to jail, I need you to take care of all of my daughter's needs, from maternity clothes, transportation to the doctor, and groceries, because she and the baby will need to eat healthy meals … Oh, and anything else she asks for, make sure she has it! Is that clear?"

"Yes, ma'am, I can do that," JB responded.

I was in shock at how my mother spoke up for me. I had never heard her speak up for herself, let alone me. But this night, I mentally gave her a standing ovation.

JB's family was well off. They were well connected and prosperous business owners in their community, church, and city leadership, respected by all in the city of Inkster. So, it would be feasible for JB to help take care of our baby and me.

★   ★   ★

From the start, I feared being a mom. When JB took me to Hudson's to shop for maternity clothes, I added pregnancy and baby books to the list and learned how babies develop and how my body would change. I decided to educate myself about having a baby and raising a kid. I read tons of books, took my prenatal vitamins, and JB went with me to my doctor appointments.

I used the pregnancy as an excuse to treat myself to Dominos' pepperoni pizza and chocolate doughnuts on many occasions. After all, I was eating for two! I indulged in the delight, as it was one of the few things that allowed me to forget about my predicament and release my sense of guilt and shame. The guilt of having let people down, especially my mother, and shame of displaying the fact that I had premarital sex and was now going to have a child out of wedlock. My predicament was so far from the dreams I had imagined for myself.

Once the word got out that I was pregnant, it was like having the plague. Friends from church avoided me; boys looked at me sideways, and one night, she called. "Is it true you're pregnant?" his ex-fiancée tearfully questioned me.

Kids on the bus were making fun of me being a church girl and having sex. The one comment that crushed my spirit was from a chubby girl who said, "I heard you're having sex with a grown man."

"Ooh, you are fast," the older girls chimed in from the back of the bus. I felt so ashamed and blacklisted.

It was the most humiliating experience I'd had. After the gang of girls had their share of teasing, a twelfth grader named Kim came and sat next to me on the bus. She held my hand. I mustered a smile.

"Don't worry; you're not alone. I'm pregnant too."

I felt I had an ally. Although we were both in the same boat, which was scary, knowing that I had a partner was comforting. "Thank God I'm not the only one in school walking the halls with big boobs and a big belly," I said.

Being in school was an altogether different story. I found myself always stressing about what someone else thought. I craved to be known as a twin and as an individual and liked by everyone, only to be the tarnished one. I stuck out like a sore thumb in tenth grade. Walking through the halls in high school was like being the center of attention, since I was one of two girls pregnant out of the entire school. Unfortunately, it didn't help my notoriety to be dressed in maternity attire. My appearance in everyone's eyes was a pregnant teenager.

Three days a week, I called JB to meet me at the bus stop to pick me up. I didn't fit in at school. He'd come racing down the street in a red T-Top Camaro and arrive just as my bus did. He was the solace I needed and when I needed it.

My pregnancy was considered high risk because I was only fifteen, but it became more manageable than I thought it would be. But giving birth was something totally different. Whoa! That pain was something I'd never felt before! But fifteen days after my sixteenth birthday, after three hours of labor, Nicole was finally born. She was a healthy nine-pound baby girl with a full head of black hair and gorgeous eyes. She was beautiful and healthy. She was mine, and she looked just like JB. There was no way he could deny his baby girl.

I couldn't wait to leave the hospital, but the second we got home, I froze. It was like, *Oh, no! I have a baby! What do I do now?* I'd never felt more lost. With help from my mom, sister, and neighbor, I gradually figured out how to care for her, feed her, and bathe her. We decorated a beautiful bedroom for her with a Minnie Mouse theme, but she slept with me every night for the first five months.

Although the reality of being a dad gave JB cold feet, he eventually came around to the idea of it and stayed in the picture. We were on excellent terms, almost inseparable. While things on the JB front seemed to be working out fine, there was conflict back home.

My stepfather didn't like the fact that JB was over to the house so much and that I'd leave for days, even weeks. It was causing problems with him and my mother. And finally, one day, Mom gave me an ultimatum.

"Get married or go live with your father."

My mother offered me only two choices. I knew I didn't want to live with my father, and I couldn't tell anyone why. I had to keep what happened to me in Las Vegas a secret. Plus, my mom wouldn't believe me and say it was my fault, so I called JB and told him the choices. He agreed to marry me.

CHAPTER

7

THE GREAT ESCAPE

On November 11, 1985, JB and I needed a way out to make it right, and I guess I thought marriage was it. I thought about the shame I'd brought on myself and my mom, and I didn't want my daughter to grow up without her father like I did. So we went along with it. I understood the choices, or I thought I did, and why my mother signed the marriage license application. I needed parental consent because I was not eighteen yet.

JB and I got married in the office of my pastor, the late Elder Jesse Ross, with our baby girl, Nicole, in our hands. JB and I became husband and wife with my twin sister and his brother Danny as our witnesses.

I was utterly unprepared for life in general or as a mother, let alone a wife, but my journey to adulthood began. I was sixteen years old, an eleventh grader at Kennedy High School, with a baby and I was married. No one could have prepared me for the twists and turns my life was about to take as a mom and wife, sacrifices that needed to be made, or the struggles and tears I was about to embark on. I had little sense of who I was. I locked my dreams of being a black woman in law enforcement or mortuary science deep within my mind and threw away the key.

I tried to remember seeing my parents being happy in their relationship, being with their new mates, and finally being satisfied, but the only pictures I had in my head were the infidelity and constant arguments.

My social life was at zero. I couldn't relate to my old friends anymore, even my classmates—the things they talked about, the clothes they wore, the places they went—and I didn't even have a driver's license. I was an outsider looking in. Gone were the New Edition posters. Instead of staying up, late listening to music or talking to my sister, I went to bed at 8:30 PM, so I could get up at 6 AM with Nicole. She was my priority now; she was my life. I was crazy about her. At fifteen months, with fat cheeks, black curly top hair, and running everywhere, she was my cute baby doll.

In no time, she was talking ... at least trying. She could utter several words. She'd say "Mama," "Mamaw" (that's what she called my mom), "bye-bye," "hi," and "pizza" was her favorite. She would wave bye-bye, clap her hands, and point at what she wanted.

Our parents helped pay for some of Nicole's stuff and for bills. My mom barely babysat, and my twin was living her own life but watched baby Nicole when she could.

Some nights, I'd put Nicole down, and she'd fuss nonstop. I tried so hard to get her to stop crying, and then Danny or his girlfriend Kim would come along and quiet her down in half a second. I must admit it, that made me feel bad.

I dropped out of school in the eleventh grade; I didn't fit, and school wasn't for me. I signed up to get my G.E.D. In my mind, a general education diploma was just as good as a regular high school diploma.

By Nicole's second birthday, I was soon to be delivering baby number two. On August 8, 1987, into the world came another bouncing baby girl, Marie. I would have another child, Yvette, on July 16, 1991.

By twenty-one years old, I was a mother of three beautiful daughters, each favoring their father and me in their own way. They were well behaved most of the time, but they had their moments like any toddler or child. Marie, who would throw tantrums and her food at restaurants, often caused us to miss out on family dinners. JB was a great dad. The girls meant a lot to him. However, he had his own character flaws.

JB's parents and extended family loved finger pointing and questioning my abilities for being a good mother. If the girls were out of line, acted up, or if they fell over and bumped their heads, I always thought people were looking at me as if to say, "It's because you're a teenager."

"You'll be nothing. You're just like your mama; she was nothing, and guess what, you'll be—nothing." Those words were spoken to me by JB's father … and he said it to my face.

Nevertheless, the whole situation from the beginning was a challenge for both of us. JB wasn't planning on having a baby, let alone a teenage wife, and I wasn't planning on having a baby or getting married, but we tried. There were times we laughed or had fun hosting cards and birthday parties. It was like climbing a mountain; unprepared, we kept falling.

"Boy, you better get out there and make my money" was JB's dad's favorite line.

I discovered that payday occurred every day when driving a

taxicab. JB's job of driving a cab for his father kept him away from home most of the day and into the night. He worked hard at supporting both of us, spending ten- to twelve-hour days, including the weekend and holidays, driving a cab for his father out of the Detroit Metropolitan Airport, making cash money with no taxes every day. But the cashflow was based on the weather, holiday season, or major entertainment events that would attract tourists and fans, causing them to fly into the airport. We were struggling financially, drowning in debt from paying the rent and buying food and clothes for our daughters.

I was lonely and felt as though I had been set up. My friend circle was small, and the friends that I had were adults. I visited more with my grandparents because they were home. My twin sister was living her best life, doing things that teenagers do, like high school sporting events, dates, and hanging out with friends. But I'd put Nicole to sleep, cut on the TV, and wait until JB got home. I blamed myself and JB for disrupting my life.

Thrown into the adult world, I worked various jobs, attempting to help make ends meet. I started out as a direct care worker, serving those with disabilities at one of JB's parents' group homes (they owned several). I worked the afternoon and midnight shifts and weekends too. Onward, I landed a gig as a makeup artist at the local Westland Mall for Cardeuix Cosmetics, approaching women of all colors to try a new shade of lipstick, eyeshadow to match their clothing, or face-lifting cream for those who were older. As a woman in my early twenties, I discovered that skincare and makeup were influential means for bringing women to life.

There was a feeling of an immediate connection to the person whose makeup I was doing. Touching their faces was up close and personal, and getting them comfortable with me became just as important as the sale. I learned that making small conversation that was focused on them while touching them was channeling energy that made it relaxing for them. Not only that, I discovered that makeup gave women a feeling of empowerment that was rewarding. It was amazing to see how something as modest as a tube of lipstick could give someone the self-confidence to do something different. There is power in conversation and touch. In an uncanny way, doing makeup gave the women a voice; we shared and laughed at life's imperfections, whether it was an oversized mole on the cheek or a birth mark or battle scar from being a victim of domestic violence. We all have imperfections as beautifully flawed survivors. Some cover them up with makeup while others hide behind hijabs and religion. I began to examine myself.

I realized JB's flaws. They were heart piercing, soul tying, and health threatening escapades that drove me to the edge of insanity—and none of it made sense. For richer or for poorer, for better or worse … We'd made vows to one another, but it seemed none of it was true. Over the years, I felt confused and torn, faced with so many thoughts about life and my decisions, questioning how I got there. I was stuck.

Although I trusted that my husband was working long hours to take care of his family, his behavior became odd, and our fights escalated further than they should have. Small stains became giant spots.

"What's all this down the front of your pants?" I inquired of JB after seeing white stains down the front of his black dress pants.

"Oh, that's ice cream that spilled while I was driving the cab."

I believed him until the dry cleaners couldn't get it out. I learned that the ice cream was really semen from a blow job he had received. He confessed. I began to cry, and my sadness turned to anger then rage. Later that evening, when JB showed up, I began to pull his clothes from the closet and throw them on the porch.

"What the hell are you doing to my suits? I had them custom made! Are you crazy?" JB yelled as he got out of his cab.

Frustrated, hurt, angry, and disappointed at JB, his family, and my family, I grabbed anything I could and threw it across the room. I didn't care anymore. It just didn't matter. I became depressed about finding out that my marriage was simply a lie. Then the secret was out of the bag; JB was spending money to feed his addiction. He was buying pussy from the streets, the clubs, and anywhere in between.

Drifting back in time, during my pregnancy with my first baby, I could clearly remember visiting my doctor for my trimester check-up.

"If you're going to have sex, you need to wear a condom."

"A condom?" I was sick to my stomach. My obstetrician told me that the vaginal irritation and burning I thought was a urinary tract infection was, in fact, a sexually transmitted infection. JB was putting the wellness of myself and our babies at risk due to his promiscuous behavior, and I was in shock.

JB's lies and unfaithfulness uncovered that he had been cheating for our entire marriage. It was as though he had an addiction, but instead of it being gambling or drugs, it was sex, from sex with his ex to women on the streets.

My mom, aunt, and cousins shared their thoughts over coffee and cake. "Get over it; it's what men do," they said. "Girl, we've all been through it."

It was crazy and insane to be blamed for what was happening in my marriage. I stayed, I cried, and prayed, desperate to make my marriage work, even through the years of abuse. I had to face it. Life does not come with a mistake-free manual. And there's no way to shred up words that we shouldn't have said or choices that we shouldn't have made.

Our relationship didn't get better; plus, I was never accepted into his immediate family or branches of the family tree, only tolerated. There was always family drama or a crisis that kept us against each other, and we never truly connected in the way that we should have as a married couple. I was embarrassed and ashamed.

The clashes and loads of accusations and the personal insults coming from my in-laws were unbelievable, and I thought they were in the church.

"You'll be nothing, just like your mother" were harsh words spoken to my face or by telephone often by my father-in-law, who claimed to have known my parents' history. "Your mama was hot in the pants, a teenage whore who broke your daddy's first marriage up," he boasted.

What the fuck? Who the hell does he think he is? I thought. *To talk about my mom and dad to my face, claiming to be a Christian, head deacon of the church.* I cried hysterically. I didn't have any support. Again, I was being compared to my mother, criticized by church people, and for what? I was being attacked with words, for which I had no defense.

I struggled with insecurities from my childhood, questioning whether I was a great mom and whether my daughters knew I was crazy about them. Living the adult life—mother and wife, teen pregnancy—believe me, it wasn't easy. My life began to blur; I couldn't focus on my daughters, let alone myself. I needed direction.

Life became overwhelming, and I was beginning to crack. There's no repairing a marriage that never really existed in the first place. I was devastated.

As our marriage began to dissolve, I found myself going back, digging through my past, scrolling through pages of life, searching for that defining story, the one that basically summed up who I was, the way I was, and how I had always seen myself. But I had so many of those moments. The fact of the matter was there wasn't just one.

The search was over; that defining moment exposed itself, and I didn't need any more questions to be answered or to look for ways to make my marriage work. It was another late night, way past three in the morning, and JB hadn't made it home from the airport. I knew that flights slowed down after eleven o'clock, meaning not many cab drivers were needed for traveler transportation. I paged him multiple times for him to call me back. But I had no luck reaching him.

I began to pace the kitchen floor. "I know there aren't any flights coming in, especially past this hour." The girls were asleep in the other room. "I bet he's out cheating like he always does." I was deeply hurt and agitated because this man couldn't stop chasing skirts, and I wasn't enough.

The years of infidelity took a toll on me. Doctors during each pregnancy recommended safe sex practices because of complications due to sexually transmitted infections. I knew I wasn't stepping out in the marriage, and there was only one person left … JB.

The manhunt was on. I didn't care about how late it was, I had to see it for myself.

"Girls, it's time to get up," I quietly said to Nicole and Marie. I needed to see him cheating for myself, and this was the night.

"Where are we going?" yawned Nicole. She was just six years old.

"Just for a ride," I whispered as she and Marie got dressed.

I dressed Yvette, who was just a baby. Coats on, snacks in hand, and blankets in tow, one by one, I piled them into my burgundy Honda Accord and drove to the Detroit Metro Airport. I went into autopilot and fell into a trance, thinking about the names I would call him, wondering if I could slap him hard enough that he would hurt as badly as I did. I imagined handling it like a movie heroine, cursing him out and then setting his cab on fire.

It was pitch black outside, with not even one star in the night sky. I could see only by the moon's faint light and the small square orange lights lining the road. As I drove down I-94, the deserted four-lane highway, going well over the speed limit, I was in a rush. My mind was racing with scenarios; I was enraged, picturing him parked in a lot, sitting in the back seat with another woman on top, seeing her grinding in pleasure.

"How dare he?" I repeated as I drove in the rain. I beat the steering wheel as a slow stream of tears traveled down my cheeks. *What does she look like? Is she pretty? Is she good in bed? Is she on top? Are they doing it from behind?* I knew my anger was intensifying, because all I could think of was getting my hands around JB's neck.

Rain pounded onto my windshield as I approached the exit; my wheels slipped a little on the wet pavement, but I kept the car steady. Peering through the front window, I was trying to see what was ahead of me. The rain was coming down in buckets, blurring my vision even more. The windshield wipers whipped back and forth over my window. I attempted to clear the fogging windows, but they weren't clearing fast enough. I had a sick sense and began to feel queasy.

I was anxious as I looked out of the side window, and in the distance, I saw a Detroit Metro cab parked in a lot underneath the streetlight. The glaring light cast a shadow, enhancing the silhouette of two people in the backseat.

The rage hit me right in the chest. I began to shake uncontrollably with anger, beating the steering wheel. I went numb, in a moment of shock as tears filled my eyes.

"Hell no!" I screamed. Racing around the curb, I maintained control of the car as it swerved. "Oh shit," I hollered as the girls' cries snapped me out of my rage.

The car made a loud screeching sound as it skidded and then came to a stop. I jumped out of the car in the pouring rain. The windows of the cab were foggy, and the doors were locked. But I could see into the vehicle through the windshield—it was JB fucking in the back seat of his cab. She was on top of him, grinding just like I imagined.

He was caught dead in the act.

"Open the fucking door, JB!" I screamed, pounding on the windows and kicking the doors. I could see him and the chick scrambling to put their clothes on. It was taking them too long. In my rage, I grabbed the lug wrench from my trunk and went to town, shattering the windshield, beating the car until it looked like a battered tin can.

I heard screams from Nicole and Marie. "Mama, Mama!" Yvette was crying. Immediately, I came to myself, drenched from my hair to my shoes. I stopped, threw the wrench back in the trunk, and sped off. My daughters and I cried all the way home … me from anger, frustration, and heartbreak, them from the fear and terror of having seen me act like a crazy lady.

My mind wasn't playing tricks on me; the vision that I had was a kind of spidey sense, that gut-wrenching feeling, that warning system I'd had since I was a kid.

Hurriedly, I got the girls into the house, and after I hung their coats up, heading up the stairs, JB burst through the front door like a mad man, grabbing my hair. I lost my balance, falling back when he dragged me down the stairs.

"Bitch, why did you destroy my cab?" he yelled. I guess he

wasn't happy with my destructive behavior in reaction to his serial cheating. He picked me up, and I grabbed his face.

"Motherfucka, I'm tired of your cheating!" I screamed and panted. I was having a meltdown. I had lost any right mind that I had left. We fought up and down the hall, into the living room where he slammed me onto the dining room table.

"Daddy! Mama! Stop!"

My legs crumbled, and we fell to the floor. I could see the girls standing on the stairs, crying. Nicole was holding Yvette, and Marie was hanging on to her.

"Go upstairs," I yelled.

When JB punched me in the face, everything went black, and I don't remember much after that.

What was missing? Something in common beyond our children. Opposites attract, no doubt, but there was nothing to sustain us as a couple after our initial physical attraction ended. I was rational, logical, and political; he was a man of few words, interested in hustling and sleeping around and didn't care for academic pursuits.

Frustration turned to pain, and I didn't want to face what I had known for a while … my marriage was over. *What was I not doing right?*

As I flipped through the pages of our seven-year relationship, I wondered what I really meant to JB. He was my teen crush, and I was just a detour for a twenty-two-year-old guy who wanted to live the life.

The attempts at making life right by trying to change situations seemed to fall apart. I inevitably failed and was pushed farther into a world where my hope became a false reality. And for every step forward, I'd fall down an entire flight of stairs. I couldn't win for losing, it seemed.

As a mother and a wife, I failed at times, under the pressure to be perfect, fighting the odds stacked up against me. Not knowing how to love others, let alone love myself. It was time for me to move. Our marriage was over. I was twenty-two years old.

CHAPTER
8

HERE COMES THE JUDGE

The summer of 1992, I filed the divorce papers. At twenty-two years old, a mother of three little girls, I would soon be free from my tumultuous marriage with JB. Looking back, we were doomed from the very beginning. He was a young man with the world ahead of him, and I was a troubled teenager with nowhere to go. We separated and I was on my own.

Wanting to give my girls a better life than me, I decided it was time for me to go back to school, follow my dreams, and show the world and the naysayers who'd said I'd be nothing that I was going to be something. And most importantly, I'd show my daughters and myself that I was somebody. I wasn't the college student who wrote letters to college to get accepted. I had a GED that allowed me to enroll into a community college, Wayne County Community College. I was excited and liberated and kept it to myself. This lifetime decision wasn't forced; there was no ultimatum for me to choose.

I wanted to get an education and beat the odds that were against me. So that summer, I applied online, requested financial aid to assist with paying for classes, and scheduled an appointment with my academic advisor for the next day.

As fast as the sunset, the morning came quickly. I met with the advisor, sharing with him my aspirations to be a mortician. He directed me to take a math assessment to see if I qualified for the mortuary science program's pre-requisites. I passed with flying colors.

"Congratulations. Here is a plan of work that will guide you in the right direction. Now you can select your classes." The advisor smiled and handed me the campus course catalog.

I enrolled as a full-time student with twelve credit hours. I took classes in pre-mortuary science to prepare me for Wayne State's School of Mortuary Science and criminal justice as a backup plan. Classes were three nights a week—Monday, Wednesday, and Thursday, 4 P.M. until 10 P.M.—and I discovered that they were all held at the Wayne County Community College downtown campus. Yes, Downtown Detroit.

Was this fate?

* * *

When the professor walked into the class, it wasn't the stride in his steps that was eye catching, but the cool limp with each step, something that he later shared came about as a result of breaking both ankles while parachuting, one of his bucket list activities. Something was alluring about him, however. In his own right, he was captivating, engaging, knowledgeable, tall, and his hazel eyes were almost like mine, except they were greener. He looked distinguished in the nice suit he wore.

At first, it was innocent. But then he stopped me in the hallway during the lecture break. "You're new to campus, aren't you?" he asked. "Where are you from?"

"Yes, I'm new to the campus. I'm from Ypsilanti, Michigan, and I'm chasing my dreams," I replied.

"I knew it! I've been teaching here for years, and I know a new face when I see one, especially a pretty one. Chasing your dreams, huh? Well, tell me about them," he inquired.

He seems quite interested in learning about his new student, I thought. But I answered his follow-up question, nonetheless. "I've dreamed of being a Detroit homicide detective or a mortician since I was a kid, and I'm finally on the journey."

"Wow, a Detroit homicide detective … That's great."

At this point in our conversation, we were interrupted by another man who had walked up. "What's up, frat?" he said to the detective.

The man quickly turned to me and said, "Hello, beautiful. I'm Commander Jones of the Detroit Police Department recruiting, and one of the college's criminal justice program professors like my fraternity brother here." He pointed at my college professor.

I was amazed, for a lack of a better word. *How could this be? The man in charge of the Detroit Police Department recruiting is standing right in front of me.*

"So, Judge, who is this beautiful young lady?" Commander Jones asked, gesturing at me.

"Her name is Ms. Antoinette. She's a student in my class, majoring in mortuary science."

"Mortuary science? Why not be the police, where you can become certified in crime scene investigation, which will pay you more?"

"I think she should go to law school and become an attorney," rebutted the Judge, also referred to as my professor.

"Nah, man, I don't think she should do that either," the young professor defended. Whispering underneath his breath, he said, "You won't have to take all those years to become a funeral home director. I can help you get into the police academy. I'm the man who can get you the job. Give me a call," he said as he handed me his business card.

"You can?" I said in awe. I was all smiles, thinking this was a dream come true.

Seemingly sensing the budding attraction Commander Jones displayed toward me, my professor cut the conversation short. "Well, the break is over. Time to go back to class."

Am I dreaming, or is it real? I could barely focus on the remaining portion of the lecture. I had a lot to think about, like changing careers and joining the police department. My dream was coming true.

* * *

The class itself was adventurous, to say the least. I looked forward to going to class. The attention I received from the Judge was enough to feed my bruised ego and low self-esteem for a decade or two. I studied hard, made sure I was prepared for each class, and was often called on to answer some of the toughest questions. I guess you can say I was the teacher's pet, so to speak. But I enjoyed every moment of it.

One day, after the lecture was over, the Judge stopped me on my way out. "Do you have a minute or two? I'd like to get you a bite to eat."

Taken aback, I paused. In retrospect, the Judge had been flirting with me from day one. Maybe he felt that since the semester was nearing an end, the professor-to-student relationship was no longer compromised. The only things left were a few more classes and the final exam. So technically, we were free to enjoy a quick meal or a drink or two, I assumed.

Recognizing my brief hesitancy, he followed up with, "Let's just go next door to Tommy's Detroit Bar and Grill."

"Sure, I guess," I answered.

I figured I had a few minutes to spare to grab something to eat. I needed a social outlet. My world had become fashioned around motherhood, work, and studying. The break was welcomed. And besides, the girls were in good care with their dad, so I wasn't on the clock.

We were greeted by the host the moment we stepped foot in the restaurant-slash-lounge. Everyone knew him. "Nice to see you, Judge," said an attractive blonde Caucasian woman wearing flared-bottom jeans.

"Good to see you too." He hugged her close.

"Your usual, Hennessy on the rocks?"

He isn't a stranger to this place, I thought.

Tommy's was near empty. It looked eccentric and mysterious too. The hanging red lights and smoke from the cigarettes clouding the room made it feel more like a den than a bar.

"I'm glad you could make it." The judge grinned. This place was known for its burgers, made with Tommy's unique season mix. "It's the best," he said while licking his lips and looking at me. I was young enough to be his daughter.

"I'm glad I could too." I wasn't sure if he was licking his lips because of his hunger or because he saw me as prey—maybe it was both.

"There's a lot of history in this building," he shared.

"Oh, really?" I said, grinning ear to ear.

"Here's your drink. Are you ready to order, Judge?" Her eyes were all on him as if I didn't even exist.

"We'll have two cheeseburgers with fries and whatever she wants to drink." She skillfully hadn't included me in her request, but he ordered my food and told the waitress, "And whatever she wants." Obviously, he had noticed the disrespect and had my back.

Perfect ten for him, I thought, cheering to myself. The Judge had seen the disrespect and stood up for me!

Is she one of his many girlfriends? I thought, based on the attitude and lack of service. I mean, the Judge was single, and whatever he was doing was none of my business. I guess he had it like that. I took the Baileys and Cream.

I could hardly see anything except for the bar, a pool table, and an old-school jukebox. This hole in the wall looked more like a poker room than a grill, with crushed green tablecloths, round tables, chairs, and chain smokers coughing in the distance. There I sat, sipping on my drink.

"It was built in eighteen hundred and forty," he said after the waitress walked off. "Has ties with a gang called the Purple Gang, a criminal mob of bootleggers and hijackers with mostly Jewish white boys. There are even tunnels from the river used to smuggle liquor during Prohibition when this was once a speakeasy."

I was totally captured by his artistic conversation and knowledge. Guess one would have to be skillful in communication being a lawyer and chief judge.

I was clinging to every word.

"You really would make a good lawyer," he said, taking a sip of his drink.

"You think so?" I asked. I had never had a desire to be stuck in a stuffy courtroom for hours every day. I wanted to move around. I loved action.

"Yes, you would. I can see you dressed in pinstriped double-breasted suits, heels, with that Halley Berry cut," he said, scanning me from head to toe. "Detroit isn't like Ypsilanti. You're a country mouse in a big city and will get eaten up," he said, trying to prepare me for the harsh reality of this place. He didn't know that nothing scared me, and no one could stop me once I put my mind to accomplishing something.

"I can help you get into law school," he promised. I was excited about the possibility. I felt fortunate and unique.

Our first date was a significant event that took on a fairy-tale value in my mind. He invited me over to his home for drinks, which led to sex. I was twenty-three, and he was forty-three, almost twice my age.

Feels like déjà vue; I've been here before, I thought to myself.

Chief Judge was twice my age, but I had a connection with him that was peppered with our sexual encounters and spirited—at times, dangerous—adventures. We shared meals, beds, and weekends. I was an adult and mature enough to consent to sex. I may have even been taken advantage of in one way or another, but it didn't feel like it. I was having just as much fun and getting just as much out of our "relationship" as he was.

We played spin the bottle in his chambers. I didn't hide the relationship with my family or friends. I introduced him to my grandfather and even took my twin over to his house for pre-Thanksgiving dinner when he bragged about being a chef. But the dinner was a disaster. He burned the cranberry dressing, the turkey wasn't done, and the mashed potatoes were lumpy.

He was amazing to me. He was a gentleman, respectful, reliable, and treated me like he really liked me, from the weekend getaways to shopping trips where he purchased my business suits, name brands, from Saint Laurent to St. John.

Summer 1993. Shortly after graduating with an associate in arts degree from Wayne County Community College and after our launch and completion of a successful criminal justice class forum titled Stopping the Gun Violence, which involved city officials and residents, the Handgun Intervention Program, known as H.I.P., was birthed. It was a 36th District Court-based education program targeting young African American men aged twelve to twenty-eight, who were first- or second-time offenders, charged with carrying a concealed weapon, currently had no other serious charges pending, and ordered to attend a four-hour session as a condition of their bond.

The program's goal was to prevent these defendants from committing gun violence or becoming homicide victims, and it stressed the importance of consequences, choices, responsibility, and nonviolence.

"Well done, Judge," I said as I sipped on a glass of champagne while we lay in bed one night. We were celebrating the program's success.

"Cheers! Thank you, Antoinette. This is only the beginning. I'm working on a book, and when I can retire, maybe I'll run for mayor. What do you think about that?"

Before I could answer, he followed with "Antoinette, I think you'd make a great lawyer … help stop some of this corruption in Detroit."

"You think so?" I asked, staring out the window at the city's darkness, halfway to my next chapter in life. "I'd rather not."

"You know they're all in this together—the police, city

politicians, and pastors. And if I were mayor, things would be different." He sighed.

Everything was going great. That is, until I asked about attending social events, award ceremonies related to the Handgun Intervention Program, or the Barristers' Ball, a black-tie fundraising event hosted by the Michigan Bar Association. I wanted to mix and mingle with those in the legal, business, civic, and political communities in Downtown Detroit at the Renaissance Center.

"Not right now."

"Why?" I questioned.

"Because you don't need to move in those circles."

"Is it that I don't need to, or you don't want me to?" I said, confronting him. "Why are you leaving me out of the loop?"

He paused for a moment and then took a deep breath. "You know I like you a lot, Antoinette." His hazel eyes looked sincere, but I could see the lies. "I don't want anyone to see us together. They'll put two and two together, and I could lose my career on the bench and as a professor at the college," he said as he gently caressed my face as if I were a child.

"Your reputation? What's to be afraid of? We're both adults, right?" I was pissed. Here I was thinking we were a couple. I had to be honest with myself. Nothing about our relationship would ever change. He valued his career and reputation over our so-called relationship.

"Is that all?" I said sarcastically.

"Plus, I'm not trying to be a father to anymore girls. I have one daughter, and that's enough."

"I never asked you to be my girls' father. They already have a father, one who's involved in their life, unlike yours," I shot back.

"I didn't say you did, but the reality is that you're a package, and with you comes them, and that's not for me." He took a sip of the cognac that was sitting on the nightstand.

I felt a surge of heat escape my ear canals. "I've been out of college for over a year, and whenever you called, I came!" I said, trying to pull a guilt trip on him. I wanted him to feel guilty for using me and leading me on.

"Antoinette, you're taking this the wrong way," he said, trying to ease the rising tension.

"The wrong way? What the fuck?!" I yelled as I jumped out of bed and scrambled to find my clothes in the moonlight.

I hurriedly dressed, grabbed my things, and left. That was the last night of my love affair with the Judge. I cried all the way home. The thoughts of regret, shame, and blame danced in my head. *How could I not see this—or did I?* I asked myself. Did I consent to sex with the chief judge … my professor? I was sure that if you asked him, he'd say the relationship was consensual and he made no promises. In other words, he did nothing wrong. But if you asked me, he misled me and, therefore, culpability rested with him.

I began to internalize and ask myself questions. Was I a victim of professional abuse and manipulation? I was devastated. Not only was I struggling to be a single parent, but I was also a single woman who was obviously trapped by her past. It had a hold on me; it was like being incarcerated but without bars, and I was about to break free, or so I thought.

Survival was all I could see as I took care of Nicole, Marie, and Yvette, let alone me—I was last on my list. I had to protect them from any danger, be it from a stranger, friend, and especially family. All I could think of was my girls; they depended on me, and I had to protect them. I didn't want them to experience what happened to me, my grief and trauma.

My life had certainly seen its share of ups and downs. I was lost and in a dark place. Then I remembered the conversation with the recruiting commander of the Detroit Police Department: *"I can help you get into the police academy. I'm the man who can get you the job. Give me a call."*

The commander's words repeatedly played in my mind as I grabbed my purse, frantically searching for his business card.

It was like a light came on, my dream of being the police.

It's not what you know; it's who you know, right? I thought to myself.

After scouring around for days, trying to locate the business card he had given me, I finally found it and gave him a call.

I excitedly re-introduced myself. "Commander Jones, this is Antoinette from Wayne County Community. I met you in the hall while speaking with Chief Judge, the young lady with dreams of being a Detroit Police homicide detective?"

"Oh, I remember you; how could I forget those beautiful eyes?" he replied. "I take it that you're ready to be the police and you're done with the Judge."

"Yes, I'm ready to be the police, and I'm done with the Judge," I agreed, but I wondered how he knew about the Judge and me if we were a secret.

After going through the humiliating yet humbling experience, I agreed to meet up with Commander Jones. I needed something from him. Giving a little to get a little wasn't a foreign concept to me. I'd done it several times over. And it wasn't going to kill me to do it one more time, especially if I was promised to get something more significant in return—a job on the police force.

The next day, as I prepared myself to meet Commander Jones, my mind raced with rancid thoughts. I was determined to do what I had to do to get to the next level. Even though I was no longer with JB, I was still entangled with him in more ways than one, always having to exchange sex with JB for extra money to get my hair done or buy outfits for the girls, even though he was their father.

"That's just the way it is," JB would say, smirking. "Mutual understanding and exchange." How unfair and manipulative. But it was our reality.

"The man is just being nice and trying to show you a good time," I heard my dad's voice say in the distance. *"Now you go and enjoy yourself … You're in good hands. I'll see you later."* I could see his eyes and the grin on his face so clearly.

"God, why me?" I tearfully screamed.

Is this a set up for a ménage à trois? I asked myself.

At that moment, pain greeted me in my life. I had nothing and needed a way out in order to follow my dreams. The pain of guilt, shame, and defeat penetrated me from head to toe, finding my most vulnerable moments. I became a victim of a monstrous beast. This beast fed off my difficulties and insecurities in life. And at this point, we had a relationship. It knew me at my best and worst, which allowed me to disconnect from myself. I couldn't escape it; it became my superpower.

Let's bring it on. I've been here before. I struggled with that internal conflict all night. I knew it was a ticket away from Ypsilanti, the church, JB, and the pain of my childhood. One night. One night with a dirty old man. One night, and my troubles would be over.

"You got this!" I told myself as I looked in the mirror, attempting to convince myself that I was prepared for whatever was next in my life.

That spring night after class felt so tropical. I walked from class to Tommy's Detroit Bar and Grill, the little burger joint across from the Wayne County Community College administration building, what we called the Cheese.

As I walked from the student parking lot to Tommy's in the darkness, I could feel the breeze that traveled from the Detroit River and could hear the music from clashing waves. I imagined myself on the beach with sand running through my toes. That is, until reality hit me. The clicks of my heels reminded me that I was tap-dancing on the sidewalk of life.

"Hey, Antoinette," a voice echoed from across the bar.

As I opened the door to the grill, there he was sitting at the bar, wearing his crumpled beige trench coat, with a inflated demeanor, smoking a cigarette. Commander Jones, a real-life Columbo. I laughed to myself.

"Well," Commander Jones said. "If you don't want to, you don't have to. I wouldn't have you do anything you're not comfortable with. I can get you in the academy in four weeks, a process that usually takes four months." He went straight to the point of our meeting, frank and honest.

"Being a police officer would be a dream come true." There was no need for clarity as to what he was referring to because I knew.

I've been here before was playing in my mind. I realized that sex was a unique qualification to get a promotion without much effort and trouble. Sex was used as a presentation to entertain those in power and control to get quickly promoted, whereas others waited based on their experience and skills, and I couldn't wait.

This was a once-in-a-lifetime opportunity. *If I do it, I won't have to worry about anything; it's that simple.* At that point, I disconnected myself.

"To the bat cave."

"The bat cave?"

* ★ *

There was a chair, a couch, a table, a lamp, and a cigarette-butt-filled ashtray. The white walls shone like a moon in the darkness, decorated like stars, with Kappa fraternity and Detroit Police insignia. The bat cave was a condo the commander and his frat brothers used as a getaway from life.

It felt like hours to get home, where I showered for days to scrub away the shame and reek of cigarette smoke from my lips and skin.

"When you lay with dogs, you get fleas." I'd heard that quote from my mother, but I didn't know that the residue takes days when you lay with a smoker. Nevertheless, as quick as he came, it was worth a lifetime opportunity.

I applied to the Detroit Police Department, and within days, I got the phone call to report for the written test. I was confident that I would succeed. This confidence took me through the multiple-question booklet. While I never took the S.A.T, this experience had to be close, and I had to pass. One by one, I blackened the answers to those I knew, and I revisited the ones I would take a wild guess on.

The test was all multiple choice. Thank God for taking college courses in criminal justice and dating the Judge, who had helped me with questions related to the city, politics, policies, and the police. The thought of me being the police became real, just as real to those who were taking the test with me. We'd all walked twelve flights of stairs to sit at grade-school-size desks and chairs in Downtown Detroit.

I got very serious about the questions at the end, those harassing, underhanded dilemmas involving police doing things in the community and within the department.

The written test was in April. I passed and so did many others. Next, came the physical exam test. I had no one to cheer me on, but all those who crossed over with me strolled inside the gymnasium, which smelled of a smelly high school locker room. Nevertheless, it was okay because we cheered for each other at the Detroit Police gym, adjacent to 1300 Beaubien—the police headquarters. Running was a breeze. I started out lying on my stomach, and when the whistle sounded, I was to my feet, racing between cones, crawling through a tunnel, and climbing over a six-foot wall to get back to the beginning point. I had been preparing for the past three weeks, but that wasn't enough time; the rope climbing burned my hands, and the 180-pound dummy drag was a struggle.

The last was the "main event." I had practiced push-ups until my arms and shoulders ached with pain. But on test day, they felt like jelly. With a wailing cry, I did it with the least number of qualifying pushups—ten. I passed! I was geeked. I was on to the next phase, although there was this distressing feeling, a self-defeating habit I had, that I shouldn't be a police officer because my marriage was on the brink of divorce, which would soon cause me to be a single mother of three young daughters, ages one, five, and nine years old. I began to wonder. Perhaps I needed to choose a different career.

I completed a psychological exam, medical exam, and a background investigation in four weeks, just like he'd said. I was up next for the oral board, the last hurdle before the academy. It was fate. I felt that my future was going in the right direction. I was going to be something.

★   ★   ★

I received a phone call. Unfortunately, I didn't make the cut. I was devastated, with tears running down my face, shaking in disbelief that my success was shadowed by my failures. The recruiter questioned my being charged with welfare fraud. A mere two-hundred-dollar scandal with food stamps had disqualified me from moving forward and achieving my dream, which had seemed to be in my reach.

Then it came to me—I was going through my divorce with JB … I was single and on welfare. I spent most of that year in school getting my associate degree. JB was over for his "Let's Make a Deal" game where I would have to perform sexual favors to get money for my daughters and me. The more sexual acts I performed, the more favors I'd get from him.

Suddenly, there was a knock at the door.

"Who's that at the door?" JB demanded to know.

I was curious myself. it was midday; the baby was asleep while Nicole and Marie were in school.

"What nigga you got coming over here?"

"You sound crazy." I laughed.

JB grabbed me right as I was getting dressed and pulled me close, staring straight into my eyes. There was a look I had never seen. The knock was continuous.

"Let me go, so I can go check!" I said as I ran down the stairs. My racing heart and sweaty palms signaled something wasn't right, and when I opened the door, I found a white stranger standing on the opposite side.

"Hi, are you Antoinette Mayes?"

"Yes, I'm Antoinette Mayes." The older white lady, with long black hair, a thin, straight nose and wearing black-rimmed glasses, introduced herself as a social worker, there to do a home visit. I can't remember her name or outfit, but what sticks in my mind was her overrun, scuffed shoes and the fact that she announced that she was a social worker and needed to do an annual home visit.

"Sure, come on in. I have nothing to hide," I lied.

After their investigation, it was disclosed that JB hadn't changed his address on his license nor his vehicle registration. Thus, although it wasn't "technically" my fault, the Department of Human Services charged me with welfare fraud. I was ordered to pay back two hundred dollars I had received in food stamp benefits. Of course, JB gave me the monies owed for the amount given in food stamps. Once the penalty was paid, I received a letter stating that my case was all clear and had been closed with the State. But it didn't matter. The penalty for not understanding the system's loopholes cost me my dream of becoming a police officer.

Can I just live my life without any judgments or ridicule? Forgive me for not knowing or living up to your expectations. I felt like I was incarcerated, having the appearance of being free but chained to others' opinions about me, questioning my choices in relationships, parenting, and who I was as a mother, lover, sibling, and myself.

From childhood to an adult, I was caught between my thoughts, planning, and executions, from sexual tactics to physical engagements, whether employment, education, or church, where I would emotionally and spiritually rehearse what I was going to say or do when confronted by situations.

For my own protection, I was sarcastic and obnoxious when physically or verbally attacked by those to whom I had to prove I was right ... or that they were wrong, to defend or claim my space.

I was judged.

CHAPTER

9

BIG CITY, BIG DREAMS

Detroit was the place to be. Big lights, big city, and big dreams. It was like a giant magnet that was drawing me. Fall 1995, after tears, heartache, and hard work, I graduated from Wayne County Community College with my associate of arts degree. Just like my professor, the Judge, had said, I was beating the odds. I was proud of myself, with all the odds stacked against me—being a teenage mother, a high school drop-out, and being told I would be nothing—I had made it. I had something to be proud of.

"I did it! Look, Mom. Look, girls!" I wanted them to see me.

As an undergraduate sophomore student in their criminal justice program, I was accepted to Wayne State University, focused on a career in law enforcement or possibly mortuary science, which was still an option. With financial aid in place, a student loan, and family housing approved, I had everything mapped out.

I announced to my parents, "I've decided it's time for the girls and me to move to Detroit." I appreciated my mom and Big Jack's support for allowing me to move back home with the girls. They were a big help, but it was time for us to make a move.

"Detroit?" my stepfather shouted. "Detroit isn't a safe place to live. How will the girls succeed in a school system that failed state test scores?"

"Don't worry, Jack, I'm going to be the police, so you don't have to worry about us," I said with confidence. *Plus, I have the Judge to protect us.* "I found a charter school for the girls not far from our place."

"Where are you going to live?" inquired my mother.

"University Towers, a new construction project for student housing. A three-bedroom, two-bathroom apartment on the Wayne State campus and walking distance to classes."

"What's the address?" Jack asked.

"Forty-five hundred Cass."

"Cass? Are you out of your mind?" he snapped back.

"What's wrong with Cass?"

"Cass in an area of Detroit filled with crime, drugs, and prostitution," he explained. "You and the girls won't be safe."

I chuckled. "Whatever." If I was ever going to make it, I had to leave Ypsilanti and my past behind … follow my dreams. It was time to live my life.

As a single mother of three daughters, used to living in a small town, I decided to move my daughters to Detroit, a city that the FBI cited as one of the most dangerous in the country.

Failure was no longer an option for me. Despite all my losses and fears, deep down inside, I never gave up on my childhood dream, and just maybe moving away was best. They say when God shuts one door, he opens another, so that's what I believed; that was the start of a new journey for me and my girls. I trusted that God would open a door for us.

Relocating to Detroit was a logical decision, but could I just uproot my daughters from the quiet country life to the big city? Yes. It was a fresh start for my three young daughters and me, who were five, seven, and nine years old at the time. The product of strategic thought, it wasn't a difficult choice to make, but a plan for new beginnings. It was a thirty-minute drive on I-94 East, not too close and not that far from their father and other family members who lived a few miles away.

Honestly, I was scared about making such a big decision. I wouldn't really know anyone, and I was worried about making it and being successful. But I had to make a move. And my girls would make new friends at our new home—University Towers, a community for Wayne State University families and their new school.

We made it to 4500 Cass and moved into our new apartment that we called home, a contemporary student-family-housing high-rise building with gold-tinted windows, located right in the heart of the campus, in an area known as Midtown. There was so much culture and diversity.

The smell of fresh paint filled the air. There was turquoise carpet in our three-bedroom, two-bathroom unit. We had security twenty-four hours a day and access with a crucial card only. I felt safe.

After settling into our new home, my daughters and I were excited and ready to explore. We discovered that we were blocks from the Detroit Institute of Arts, Detroit Science Center, main public library, and Downtown Detroit during our adventure. There was so much culture right at our fingertips, and the timing couldn't have been better; we experienced the Detroit Art Festival, which boasted blocks of arts and crafts for the girls, music, and food. Then we went to Dally in the Alley, where there was more art, more people, and more diversity, which was a breath of fresh air. I knew I was in the right place.

New life, new school. I enrolled the girls into Dewey Elementary. Nicole was in the fifth grade and Marie was in third grade. Yvette walked with me and attended head start on the Wayne State campus. College mates, who were also residents of University Towers with their children, assisted me in attending classes that were within walking distance. Success was on our side.

I was very aggressive about the dreams I had for myself and my life in Detroit, not intimidated. Neither was I insecure but excited and openly shared that I wanted to be the police or even a mortician, to be the one to make a difference in the city!

As a small-town girl from Ypsilanti in the big city, my dreams were really coming true. The college campus was alive with students racing from classes to the dining hall and library and the different fraternities and sororities, recruiting, stepping, and raising community awareness for the Red Cross or having a blood drive.

The university experience was utterly different than community college. My classmates at the university were mostly Caucasian, single, and carefree eighteen-year-olds fresh out of high school or in their early twenties, and second- or third-year students. I was the twenty-five-year-old who had been exposed to life's reality versus those who had yet to live. At the community college, we all worked during the day, had children to attend to afterward, and we shared life's journey of choices, consequences, and lessons. But for some reason, I just couldn't seem to fit in at the university.

I talked to my mother every day, and she always had a word of encouragement. She always reminded me to keep God first, take care of my girls, and continue to strive toward education.

"Would you like to donate blood?" I heard a male voice say.

He was super handsome, a Sigma fraternity brother fundraising for the Red Cross. His welcoming smile was dressed in teeth that were big and white and kissable full lips accented by a trimmed mustache and beard. He wore a blue jean white-striped baseball cap, a blue jean shirt, and a sea shelled necklace with diamond earring studs in both ears and a silver thumb ring. Yes, he was wearing all that. I paid attention.

"I would, but I'm on my way to find out about my financial aid," I replied. "By the way, can you direct me to the office?"

My financial aid hadn't been posted to my account; it was the fifth of the month, rent was due and so was tuition. On top of it, I needed to purchase my books. I needed my money.

I made it to the accounting office and was told to sign in and wait for an advisor. Thank God I didn't have to wait long to be seen. Being a full-time student, with thirteen credit hours for the criminal justice program, was like working a nine-to-five, juggling homework and family, and trying to have a social life with little support. It was overwhelming.

"Come on, girls. Let's take a ride." While on a field trip to Northland Mall, outside of the city, sampling the perfumes smells, I bumped into the handsome guy I'd met on campus. I was speechless.

And there was chemistry. It was heart-pounding, stomach-laughing, panic-attack-on-aisle-ten chemistry.

He asked, "Are those your sisters?" pointing at my girls.

"Oh, no," I said, chuckling. "These are my daughters, Nicole, Marie, and Yvette. And girls, this is Hassan."

From the moment we'd met in the hallway to the moment we

reconnected, Hassan and I had a special connection. There was something different about him, more so than any of the other men I had dated. Maybe it was rooted in our vastly different nationalities or our backgrounds. I was Christian and Hassan was Muslim. Now, while our faiths were different, we were drawn to each other, and regardless of the difference, it brought us together.

★   ★   ★

In a matter of days, Hassan invited me and the girls over to his mother's house for dinner. We felt so right meeting each other's families.

As we drove north on Woodward, passing the Boston Edison District, toward West Chicago to Webb, I was in love already, not with Hassan but the neighborhood. The homes were beautiful, big, and historical, each one unique in its own architectural design. Dream homes lined the streets.

How quickly the scenery changed in just a matter of blocks, and one house stood out the closer we got to our destination—it was Hassan's mother's house. From outside, the huge house looked ready to be condemned. It sat beside a huge space, and it was leaning to the left, with concrete blocks holding up the porch. The bedroom windows, covered with garbage bags, were accented by beautiful magnolias blooming from the porch; the house was broken. The house next door belonged to her oldest daughter and five grandchildren. The crazy thing is that her daughter's house looked just like her mother's, identical in size, build, model, and landscape; it even had the same lean. Her house was broken too.

"We're here, girls," I nervously announced after parking the car and being greeted by Hassan.

"Come on in. I'm glad you guys made it!" He smiled and pressed his wet lips on mine. He was fine as they come, with white pretty teeth, full lips, a chiseled face touched by a groomed beard, and piercing brown eyes that matched his diamond earrings.

Inside, it smelled like Thanksgiving and looked a lot like Frankenmuth. A narrow, wooded hallway lined with a China Cabinet filled with black art figures guided us through the home, past the living room and dining room, which was graced by a white piano and lots of angel figurines, children of color and beautifully shaped ceramic vases, bowls, paint and paint brushes, and a multitude of ornaments and art supplies.

Hassan introduced us to his mother, sisters, brothers, and a host of nieces and nephews. It was like a family reunion or engagement dinner before the wedding day, except it was only his family. I felt accepted almost immediately, and not just me; I felt my daughters were accepted as well.

Hassan's mom, Ms. AnnMarie, was a retired social worker, having worked at Child Protective Services. She was a former school-teacher and held a master's degree in ceramics. She created beautiful vases of all shapes, sizes and beautifully decorated them with butterflies. Hassan's mother was sharp, educated, and well-spoken. Her stature didn't limit gifts and abilities; they shined through attractively and innovatively through her art.

She was the union rep, who advocated analyzed, planned, implemented, and evaluated issues of concern, not only to the local union but also for her family. She shared life stories as a black woman raising four children on her own, driving to Ann Arbor to the University of Michigan, where she was an all-A college student who obtained her bachelor and master degrees in social work and had dreams of going back to earn a Ph.D. in education.

Even though we were twenty years apart, we could relate; our struggles were the same. We were the mothers who fought our way through just to make sure our family survived. Immediately, I loved her like she was my mother.

After sharing her life's journey of being a survivor of abuse, raising her children on her own, going to college, and working two jobs, she became my hero. Ms. AnnMarie was also raising some of her grandchildren in the house, and the others were in and out.

"My house is a revolving door to them grandkids next door."

I could see having them there made her heart happy.

Hassan was her baby. "You know he's my favorite," she said as her face lit up with pride and joy.

Hassan was a mama's boy, who, at the age of thirty-one, lived in the basement of his mother's house. In my world that was a sign of danger: *"You'll never be good enough."* But my marriage was the opposite; JB's father was the culprit.

*   *   *

The realization of priorities and responsibilities were too much to bear. In the art of juggling life, no one told me that it was okay if the balls dropped; it's a crucial part of learning to juggle.

The game I'd come to acknowledge was no longer fun. Before I knew it, my grades began to slip, so did my status as a full-time student; I was now part-time, and I was placed on academic probation and sent to Detroit's Work First program, a state-required program to receive job training or else I'd lose my cash and food assistance.

"I don't need job training. I'll go find me a job," I insisted to Hassan one Friday afternoon while my girls were in school.

"Ann, you've got to think from the neck up," he would often say.

Hassan's ridiculing was next level, and I just couldn't ever get past it with him. It was like there was this invisible wall, and no matter how hard I tried, I couldn't get through, even when it came to my wardrobe.

"Why do you always wear fitting tops and sheer shirts? The way you dress is too revealing."

"What's wrong with my fitting tops and sheer shirts?" I asked as I rubbed on my breasts. "I wear a supportive bra for these D cups and tank top if needed. I think I enhance them very tastefully."

"Most of the women I know don't dress that way," he said.

"So tell me … just how do the women in your life dress?" I said with a hint of sarcasm.

"Plain and simple. Jeans and not revealing t-shirts."

"Well, this is the way I dress. I don't see anything wrong with it," I defended.

"The way you dress is a distraction and getting you the wrong attention." His eyes scanned me up and down slowly. "Do you ever look in the mirror?"

"That's insane," I snapped back. "And fuck you for saying it. I'm not Muslim; I don't wear a hijab and cover up from head to toe. I will continue to enjoy my bacon and toast. You don't really know me," I cried.

I was in tears at this point. I questioned his time and judgment. I was breathless. Finally, I got it—the oil and water comparison.

Nevertheless, I called him.

"Hey, Ann, what's up?" he answered.

"I need help finding a job," I said. "Can you ride out on the bus with me?"

"Sure, I can. Give me about an hour." He laughed.

"It's not funny!" I said.

He was laughing at my struggles and enjoying the fact that, despite our relationship issues, I had to call him for help. He knew the city and bus routes better than me. Together, riding city transportation from Cass and Woodward to Detroit's New Center area, I was glad Hassan was with me; he supported me and helped me find a job.

The bus stopped at the corner of West Grand Blvd. and the New Center Area, where we walked several blocks, passing the St. Regis Hotel, General Motors Building, Fisher Building, and a brand-new building called Fitness Works that had a sign posted on the door: Now Hiring. That was my sign, and I needed to look no further.

The next thing I heard behind me was, "Welcome to Fitness Works" from a white guy who introduced himself as John, the club's manager. "Looking for a job?" John smiled.

"Yes!" I smiled, introducing Hassan and myself. "Hi, I am Antoinette. I noticed the sign on the door: Now Hiring."

"Come with me."

The three of us walked inside the club, which was filled with hectic liveliness—construction workers drilling, pounding, and polishing and the designer in a frenzy because she had ordered twelve dozen yellow roses, not red. The pool was being filled and lockers were stacked in place.

"Our club opens in a couple of days," said John. "We're short staffed, and construction isn't even finished in the bathrooms and sauna." He sounded frustrated. "The position is for a front desk receptionist to greet guests and make sure the members feel welcome. Think you could do that?"

"I sure can," I replied.

"Here's the application. Have a seat and fill it out."

After I completed and handed back the application, John asked, "How about a tour to get familiar with the place?"

"Really?" I asked, looking at Hassan with excitement.

We followed John into a spectacular state-of-the-art fitness club. The purples, teals, and mustard yellows of the paints and carpet decorated the first floor, home to all the modern fitness equipment and high-tech physical rehabilitation equipment, which would also be home to Detroit's professional athletes. It was an escape away from the hustle of city life.

During the tour, John shared what to expect. "This new facility is Detroit's first health and wellness center and corporate fitness gym, an exclusive membership for Henry Ford and General Motors employees and their contractors, offering personal training, massages, aerobic classes, and sports leagues."

As John guided us through the club, he showed us the indoor pool, hot tub, therapeutic aqua tub, and the locker rooms.

"You guys gotta check out the second floor," he said as he jogged up the steps. The second floor had an indoor track, two racquetball courts, a full-size basketball court, and a state-of-the-art aerobic room with floor-to-ceiling mirrors.

"This is amazing." I beamed as my voice echoed.

"This is great, even for ballroom dancing." John laughed oddly.

"Ballroom dancing ... never thought about that."

"So, you live here in Detroit?"

"Yes, I moved here from Ypsilanti to attend Wayne State University."

"What's your major? What are your plans?"

"I'm in my junior year, majoring in criminal justice. Had dreams of being a cop or mortician, but I'm back at the drawing board."

"Something tells me that you have great customer service experience."

"I've helped hundreds of women pick their favorite shade of lipstick and eyeshadow; I love working with people," I offered.

He laughed. "Okay, Antoinette, I have a feeling you will be a significant part of the Fitness Works Team."

I smiled. "When do I start?"

"Have a great weekend. See you on Monday, five fifteen a.m."

"Five fifteen!" I happily replied.

"Congratulations, Ann, you got the job." Hassan smiled and hugged me as we walked to the bus stop.

I felt relieved, and on the way home, Hassan and I discussed him helping me with the girls. "If I do, can I stay with you, come over after I get off work and out of class?" he asked.

"Yes, and let's see if we can work things out too."

We both agreed.

10

FITNESS WORKS

From the outside, Fitness Works, an elaborate fitness club, resembled a glass vase, but instead of it being filled with flowers, it was a place for men and women seeking health and wellness. Fitness Works was nothing like anywhere I had ever worked before.

Opening day was like going to see the Detroit Tigers during their spring opener. It was a fun, festive party and atmosphere for Detroiters. There was everything from DJs and live music to games, raffles, food, water, Gatorade, and more.

I did everything from checking the members in to scheduling massage appointments, reserving racquetball court times, ordering for the food bar, checking the fitness equipment, to signing up new members. I was hiring, managing staff, and firing them too. John trusted me; he knew I could run the front desk.

Several months later, Detroit's downtown YMCA, the country's largest fitness facility, was scheduled to be demolished to build the new Detroit Tigers stadium, leaving its club members with no place to go.

One group was adamant about joining Fitness Works, the "Black Businessmen Club" of the YMCA, consisting of Detroit's elite and distinguished professional black men. Judges, doctors, lawyers, accountants, dentists, pharmacists, principals, teachers, CEOs of black-owned construction companies, and members of various law enforcement agencies were without a place to work out and meet.

What kind of strategic and indirect, subtle, or maybe unintentional act of discrimination is this? I asked myself. This was a time I could remember experiencing racism so blatantly in Corporate America.

I knew what I had signed on to do; I was the key, the Harriet Tubman to the Underground Railroad of corporate racism in health and fitness. I would be the way for black men to become members, and with proper documentation, I signed up all the black businessmen with level III memberships, where they could have a locker, uniform, and towel.

One of their members was a civil rights icon, Damon Keith, a giant of American law. He was committed to using the law to correct injustices as a federal judge. He was committed to working out every morning.

"Good morning, Judge!"

"Good morning, Toni." He smiled. "Toni, I'll be out next week, going out of town to speak at an NAACP event where I'm being honored and receiving an award for my work and dedication to civil rights." He shared many stories about his life, from his days in the service to witnessing Detroit's deadly riots in 1967 and beyond. I appreciated that. He was a legend.

I was from a completely different world to them. What seemed like once-in-a-lifetime opportunities to me—the Super Bowl,

All-Star Game, and NBA Finals, traveling to the islands, parties, and yacht trips—had become my reality. Their friends were famous entertainers and athletes, millionaires, and socialites. I was invited to so many of the Businessmen's Club parties, events, and trips that I lost count, but I enjoyed the ones that I made. They were like their own fraternity. They had their own rules; they even had their own language.

Some members made sure my daughters had plenty of Christmas presents under the tree, gifts for their birthdays, and backpacks filled with school supplies. There was nothing that we needed. I was grateful. The Black Businessmen's Club even surprised me with a birthday party at the Northern Lights Lounge, a bar around the club's corner. What a night to remember! The lounge was filled to capacity with club members to celebrate me, showering me with gifts and money, appreciation, and shared words and accolades for being the key, the underground access that gave them back their bond and brotherhood in a healthy and safe space.

There was a time in my life when I was an outsider. I would listen to everybody reminisce about their lives, both professional and personal, and be excluded from joining the black elites. But this time, I was a part of something bigger than myself, and I felt good about it.

Two years and two thousand club members later, what was supposed to be a part-time job became a full-time position, managing the front desk staff and sports bar. With extended hours and extra shifts, I put my educational goals on the back burner and spent more time away from home. My girls could come to work with me if I had to close. They'd sit in the food bar area, have dinner, do their homework, and play in the New Center Park, where I could see them from the desk to make sure they were safe.

I loved greeting the members. I was so good that I knew each member by name, and they appreciated that. I knew their anniversaries, children's birthdays, even some of the members' most personal stressors with their mates.

I learned that cordial small talk with members became an indepth dialogue and conversation related to anything occurring in the world and their lives—the success of promotions, new careers, salary increases, graduations, weddings, and new additions to the family. I learned of their struggles: the layoffs, separations, divorces, deaths in the family, even pets.

I was like the bartender of Fitness Works but without the drinks. As club members shared their personal lives, I shared mine, and they provided support and positive feedback, like, "Stay in school," "Get your degree," "Education is priceless," "Go see the world and don't get married," and "Enjoy single life." I pondered the conversations and felt that a change was coming.

Hassan and I continued to have conflict and heated debates about our personal and religious differences. Plus, my mom, Jack, Carlitos, and even JB questioned my attraction and attachment to a grown man who lived between my house and his mother's basement. My relationship with Hassan had hit a roadblock.

I was, again, at a crossroads in my life; it was time to weigh the pros and cons, everything from my job to staying with Hassan or breaking up, or just taking a break.

In my frustration, I cried out to God. "God, please give me an answer to my dilemma." After I prayed, I cried myself to sleep.

The next morning, I went to work. "Good morning, Dave, Brenda, Tom," I said as I scanned each of their cards. When I scanned the card of a particular member, Mike, I happened to look at the screen, and it read "Wayne County Medical Examiner's Office."

No way! This can't be real, I thought to myself; I was closer to my dream of being a mortician by way of the morgue.

"You work for the Medical Examiner's Office?" I asked Mike while handing him his workout uniform.

"Yes, I do. I'm the administrator," he replied.

"Can I talk to you before you leave?"

"Sure, Toni," he said as he walked away to workout. I was ecstatic and smiling. God was answering my prayers and opening a door.

About an hour later, Mike stopped by the front desk on his way out just like he said he would. I inquired about a position at the morgue and was delighted when he told me there was an autopsy technician position opening within two weeks. He told me he'd decide when I'd meet the chief medical examiner, a man by the name of Dr. Woo.

I could hardly contain myself during the duration of my shift that day. All I kept thinking about was my dreams coming true and taking care of my daughters without reliance on men.

There was a stark difference between embalming dead bodies and dissecting them to find out their cause of death. As a kid with big dreams and an adult with many failures, this was something I wanted … well, not exactly, but close to it. *I can do this. I was built for this; it's who I am.* It was about more than just existing at this point in my life, but to be present, living on purpose, following my dreams. And I was up next.

When I walked through those doors of the Wayne County Medical Examiner's Office, I had only one shot for one position, to make an impression on the chief in charge: Dr. Woo.

Two days later, Thursday arrived, and I was ready. On a crisp, sunny morning, as the frost-covered grass crunched under my feet, I arrived in the parking lot of the Wayne County Medical Examiner's Office at 1300 East Warren. I was to meet with Mike, the administrator, in the lobby of the morgue. It was eight A.M. sharp.

I entered through the revolving doors. The black slate floors were as dark as night, accented by white walls and ceilings with tracked lights that shined like stars. I'd transitioned from sunny blue skies to inside a room full of emotional grief and trauma, like dark gray clouds, in a matter of minutes. Groups of African American men and women were huddled in pockets everywhere I turned. They appeared distressed, some dressed in pajamas, wearing house slippers. I could see the sadness as they silently shed tears, clutching tissue boxes in their hands. I also noticed another man nervously pacing and talking on the phone. "I haven't identified Johnny yet," he said.

Another couple was hugged up, sitting close on the black leather sofa. I had to shake it off quickly. In front of me, I saw a bright light.

"Good morning. I'm George, and how may I help you?" the young African American man sitting at a white desk said as he greeted me with his warm smile.

Smiling back, I replied, "Hi, my name is Antoinette. I'm here to see Mike for a tour."

Within minutes, Mike walked out from a big white door to my left. "You ready?" he excitedly asked.

"Yes, sir," I replied as he opened the substantial white door. I crossed through and entered another dimension. The stench of death hijacked my sense of smell; rotten meat and roadkill flooded my nostrils. I had to take a couple of steps back as we walked across the black slate floors, and I whispered, "We're not in Kansas anymore."

Mike chuckled. "You're right, and I like your sense of humor. The Wayne County Medical Examiner's Office performs more than fourteen hundred forensic investigations of unexpected, violent, and suspicious deaths each year," he explained. "We handle more cases than most others in the country."

I looked at Mike and asked, "Fourteen thousand investigations?" Mike guided me through the corridors. "What in the world is this?" I said, gasping in disbelief at the datum.

"Welcome to the Spitz Museum Hallway, a collection of death-related artifacts started by forensic pathologist Werner Spitz. Spitz, who was a legendary and former chief medical examiner, collected these tools from suicide investigations and what not. Shall we continue?"

As the tour continued, we passed a glass case mounted on the wall with shelves. There was a faded newspaper clipping reporting about a worker at Better Made Potato Chip factory who had lost the tips of his fingers in an accident. A bag of chips with fingertips that had been found in a customer's bag was also on display. Another shelf displayed half-melted, crushed eyeglasses from a car crash. A baby's charred shoe found in a house fire.

There was an entire row dedicated to surgical mistakes. A fleshy blob floated in a jar of formaldehyde with a clamp attached to it; it looked like a chicken breast.

"It's a woman's breast. After a breast reduction, the doctor left the surgical clamp inside and she died months later from an infection connected to the metal instrument."

We passed remains of mutilated fetuses submerged in glass jars filled with fluid. There was another display of suicide notes, some handwritten and others typed; all were signed with love. It seemed crazy that someone who had ended their life would end a letter with a powerful word yet leave those behind to mourn.

Onward we continued, passing an office filled with cubicles. "These are our investigators," Mike said. "Meet Marc, Barbara,

Sam, Bobby, and Knight, who are retired Detroit Police and Wayne County sheriffs, except for Marc—he started back in the eighties as an autopsy technician and worked his way to the position. They go out to the scenes or locations of the deaths to collect various items such as prescriptions, jewelry, identification, and clothing."

The sounds of saws and banging hammers filled the room like an auto mechanic shop, and the odor of rotten meat and roadkill were more potent than before when we approached another white door.

"You ready?" Mike asked. "You sure you're ready?"

I looked at Mike. "Yes, I'm ready."

"Let's go. Ladies first. Welcome to the post room," he said as he pulled the white door open.

Not knowing what to expect, I slowly walked into the post room, and what I saw next was like *the X-Files, the Twilight Zone,* and *the Outer Limits* all in one, where the strange and unexplained science-fiction anthologies and aliens hit me dead smack in the face. The post room was so cold that it sent chills through my body. It felt like an electrical current, and, immediately, I had fallen into another dimension. I was face-to-face with death.

In the autopsy room, blood was everywhere. Blood streamed down the troughs that surrounded each table. About a dozen naked bodies were lying on metal trays, with toe tags hanging on the big toes like jewelry. Their heads were propped on blocks, their skulls cut and faces peeled. Their brains were removed, and organs and blood were everywhere. It was like a slaughterhouse.

About eight people were dressed in full hazmat-type bodysuits and wore masks, some working on the bodies, removing and handling different organs, weighing them, measuring them, taking samples, and replacing them in the open corpses.

I observed a person sewing the chest of a body with a needle and thread as if sewing a button on a shirt. Another person was putting a corpse in a large white body bag, feet in first, then turning him on his side while maneuvering the load underneath the body. The person wrote bold numbers from the toe tag onto the body bag's bottom with a black marker.

"We get all types of death victims: homicides, suicides, stabbings, burns, tragic accidents, men, women, and children. Death does not discriminate," Mike explained as he pointed to the bodies that resembled life-like mannequins.

Another guest entered the post room with Mike and me, a short Asian man who introduced himself as Dr. Woo, the chief medical examiner.

"I hear you have dreams of being a mortician. Do you think this is something you can do?" he asked. "We complete more than three thousand autopsies per year."

"Yes," I replied. "I've dreamed of being a mortician since I was a kid, taken pre-mortuary science classes, and always wondered about life and death. I won first prize for many of my science projects related to the life cycle of bugs and animals," I responded confidently while my palms were sweating.

"Stay as long as you like, and it's a pleasure to meet you," Dr. Woo said, smiling and shaking his head as he exited the room.

"I think he likes you; it must be those eyes." Mike smiled.

I'm sure he does, I thought to myself.

"I'll call by the end of the week to let you know if the job is yours."

Being up close and personal with death that day and seeing a person be condensed to just a shell with skin, I felt a paradigm shift that changed my perspective on life's realities.

The next day, I got a call. The only words I remember were, "You've got the job. It's yours if you want it.".

"I got the job!" I screamed with excitement.

"Yes. And orientation is next week. You'll start the following Monday." He paused before continuing. "Welcome to the team."

I cried happy tears; God had answered my prayer. That day, I gave John my resignation letter, thanking him for believing in me and entrusting me with the front desk and holding down the club.

Surprisingly, my days and nights at the club had furthered my Detroit education. Every shift, I was awake and aware, being able to watch businessmen hook up, make deals, and sign contracts verbally during a racquetball game or on the basketball court. I didn't make a lot of money, but the Fitness Works family and Businessmen's Club took care of my family and me.

Through my long working hours and different shifts—mornings, noon, and evenings—I was completely tired. But I discovered that I had resilience when it came to serving people, and no matter how busy or tired I was, I never said no to my job, and it wasn't in vain.

CHAPTER

11

THE DETROIT MORGUE

Most people know about autopsies from popular television crime dramas like *CSI* and *Bones,* with their Fantastic Four forensic teams and gadgets so radical they bordered on science-fiction. But it would soon become my reality.

In spring 1998, flowers blossomed, kissing the early morning sun on the face of the waking earth. It was sweet, like raw honey. It reminded me of fabric softener on sheets, a fresh-bed-linen scent; the fragrance was in the air. I was alive. The birds chirping in the trees sounded like a symphony of whistles and tweets. But the pleasantries of nature would quickly turn into the chambers of horrors and death when I answered the call.

Life seemed surreal. In a matter of two weeks, my salary increased, and my shift was consistent. I was working five days a week, from 8:30 A.M. until 4:00 P.M., and the benefits were terrific: a generous 401k match and full medical services, including dental, with 100 percent coverage for orthodontics, which now meant that my daughters, Nicole and Marie, could get braces. With the help of the Businessmen's Club members, I moved myself and my daughters into our new place: 3641 Russell, a beautiful three-bedroom apartment in walking distance from Eastern Market and minutes away from the hustle of Downtown Detroit.

Let the autopsies begin. I was an autopsy technician with the Wayne County Medical Examiner's Office, known as the Detroit Morgue, working in a dark room where death exposed life. I was behind the scenes of life itself and one of the Fantastic Five, a team of autopsy technicians.

On the first day on the job, I was provided with scrubs, shoe covers, and a locker number. I was instructed to change and put on a bonnet and shoe covers before entering the post room. No more club apparel, sitting at the front desk happily greeting members, or the sounds of steel hitting the floor and Motown music.

While changing into my scrubs in the employee locker room, I was overcome by an intense feeling of morning sickness, nausea, dizziness, and hallucinations. I broke out into a sweat. I prayed, asking God to take it away. It was the same feeling that had come over me at ten years old when visiting my dad in LA, except this time, it was more intense.

Once in the post room, I entered another dimension, another world. A place where life, as I knew it, would open a gateway, a type of portal between heaven and hell, dark and gray, a divided plane containing the forces of light and darkness. It was absolute pandemonium. There lay those who had been visited by the Grim Reaper, whose deaths needed exploring due to the suspiciousness of their demise, be it homicide, suicide, suffocation, hanging, drowning, gun and gang violence, beatings, stabbings, and accidents.

Had I been destined since childhood for this

life-spiritual-dimension assignment, where I dove into an astronomical experience? When my spirit, soul, and body were completely aligned with divine will and in harmony and balance ...

God, the omnipotent, had me where he wanted me to be; he was about to show me that I was in a battle between good and evil.

We are fearfully and wonderfully made. I've never seen bodies sit up or walking before collapsing, but I noticed that death has no respect for color, sex, or social status, which kept my reality in check.

I was one of five autopsy technicians. There were three other black women and one white guy. We were all aspiring to be something in life, from morticians to doctors, nurses, funeral home directors, and homicide detectives, and the morgue was a detour on our journeys. We were brilliant black women and had our own battles, from passing midterms, paying back student loans, to being single parents and raising children while fighting to keep our own dreams alive.

The smell of rotting flesh and the scent of death was abominable. It was an extremely foul odor that saturated absorbent objects, including carpet, subflooring, walls, and even my own skin, clinging like static to my clothes, resting on my nostrils' hairs.

Bodies found in the water were called floaters. Their skin was green and slipped off like a glove, a combination of gluey, slippery human slime, bloated with gasses. They resembled the *Creature of the Black Lagoon.*

Room temperature impacts the preservation of the body. During the summer's sweltering heat, the flesh was melted to mush or mummified in the winter. Coagulated, clotted blood settled in the body cavity from internal bleeding, resembling a canoe filled with water. The smells of rotten ground beef and roadkill was so overwhelming that it seeped into the skin. It took hours of showers to get rid of the smell.

It wasn't the medical examiner who performed the autopsies at the morgue; it was the other autopsy technicians in for the day and me. As an autopsy technician, I was part of a team, assigned individual caseloads and alternate days for victims of unknown causes of death, whether homicide, suicide, or accident.

We were behind the Wayne County Medical Examiner's Office scenes, and by the end of my first week, Dr. G. had nothing on me.

That first week, I did more than move bodies from the cooler to the autopsy table to the freezer and back again. I removed clothing, cleaned bodies, and bagged clothing and valuables from those who had died from being shot, beaten, raped, stabbed or committed suicide by pulling the trigger of a shotgun or hanging from a noose.

I was trained to draw fluids from the eyes and blood from the femoral artery and then X-ray the body, searching for evidence. I would dig through ripped flesh and ponds of blood to locate the bullet and shrapnel as evidence for law enforcement to get the shooter. God forbid if the deceased had a bullet lodged in the face. I would have to remove the brain and cut through the skull, into the facial bone without disfiguring the corpse. He or she was someone's family member, and I cared about that.

"The tongue is a small thing, but powerful. A great forest can be set on fire by one tiny spark" (James 3:5).

When doing a full autopsy, *all* the inside neck structures are detached, including the trachea, esophagus, and tongue. I accessed this through the chest cavity and the "Y" incision. This was done on the cases that required a full autopsy. While the tongue is the smallest organ in the body, it was one of the most challenging parts of doing an autopsy for me, having to reach up through the chest and blindly cut out the tongue, feeling around the jawbone with my scalpel. The muscle and veins were tangled like a string of Christmas lights. In the beginning, it always took me ten cuts or more to carefully cut it loose, and once free, I could hold the tongue and entire organ block. Then I was trained to close the incisions on the body, it was like sewing a tear on a shirt, except I was piecing the skin together for closure. Then I would bathe and prepare the body for release to the funeral home.

After the last autopsy, we each had chores, such as cleaning our own table, equipment, and the post room.

For those who lived closet lives, from local celebrities to the police and everyday people, their secrets would be revealed in the strangest and most tragic causes of death. One case was a gentleman, a famous local radio personality who died of strangulation when he fell from a chair. Falling from a chair isn't a rare cause of death, but it is when the man is dressed in women's clothing. He wore a dress, a bra filled with water balloons in each cup, a blonde wig, eyeshadow, blush, and lipstick, stockings, and high heels. His eyes protruded from their sockets like a goldfish, and his mouth was agape, forced open by his swollen tongue. His attire didn't kill him. It was only part of his story, but what he was engaging in up until his death was another story. While sitting on a chair in his closet, he'd tied his penis and testicles into a stocking, for what is called "cock and ball torture." Then he'd tied the stocking, which was connected to the bar, around his neck.

"Ouch! How painful." *What the heck?*

I learned that those who were into that kinky *Shades of Grey* kind of sex viewed it as a form of power exchange, literally giving up control of the penis and testicles to another person, not to cause damage, but to enhance pleasure through the introduction of temporary pain. Guess he was in a struggle within himself, and when he reached the moment of climax, the chair he used for leverage slipped from underneath, causing him to choke to death. What a way to come out of the closet and an unfortunate way to go, in a horrible freak accident. Poor guy.

One Friday night, a young man told his wife that he and the fellas were going to hang out, have some drinks, and watch the game. But he was actually taking his girlfriend out on a date. Unfortunately, they were involved in a tragic car accident. The impact of the crash set the car on fire, burning the victim to a black crisp beyond recognition. His wedding band was the only way his wife could identify her husband. I thought about his poor wife. What a way to find out your mate was cheating. And the girlfriend? Miraculously, she survived and was able to escape the burning car by climbing out the window.

Drug overdoses were expected, and in one particular case, drugs were hidden in the dead man's intestines, stomach, and esophagus. He was a drug mule who had arrived from overseas to deliver cocaine by swallowing packets of drugs, a common way that smugglers tried to move illicit substances from country to country. He was found in the bathroom of his motel on Telegraph Road. There were 236 plastic balloons of cocaine in his stomach and intestines. What a dangerous and death-defying existence, but how dangerous was it, and was it possible to survive a rupture? This guy found out the hard way.

"I wonder whatever happened to those drugs?"

In the next case, a woman in her late twenties committed suicide in the Detroit River by wearing a backpack full of books. She was found shortly after and didn't have much bloating due to the submersion. Upon investigation, we discovered that she had a lung infection, and her right lung had crumbled into yellow liquid. We removed 1.5 liters of yellow fluid from her chest cavity. Meanwhile, her left lung was fine. It was determined after looking at her medical records that she had been to the doctor's office multiple times before committing suicide; the infection had been persistent for almost a year. Several doctors had overlooked it.

The stories from those who knew her assumed that she'd killed herself to stop the pain. It was very heartbreaking. My question was how could the doctors miss the lung infection? It's sad; maybe the young lady would still be alive if they'd caught the disease in time and gave her antibiotics.

In another case, a young man in his late teens who was selling drugs was shot in a field and left to die from his injuries. The insane part was that when his body was discovered, it was surrounded by a pack of dogs that had eaten all his exposed skin, which included his face. Cats and dogs are essentially hunters, but still, dogs are thought of as "man's best friend." It's a reminder that, at the end of the day, they're still meat eaters, and as a wild pack, they will do whatever it takes to survive. It's scary and unfortunate to think of the agony the young man suffered as he passed away.

There were infants and children who died from neglect, abuse, or accidents. In one case, there was a two-year-old boy. My job was to separate him from his flesh, and because of how small he was, it took about an hour or so. He was a victim of abuse at the hands of his mother's boyfriend, whom she had only dated a month. She'd left them together for a weekend, so she could go out of town on a girl's trip. After removing the child's brain, one of the pathologists asked if I'd remove the eyes as a histology sample to perform a genome test. So I had to cut the eyes out of a two-year-old boy. I remember pulling the histology jar with my right hand while making eye contact with my left hand because both eyes looked directly into my own. I nearly passed out. An autopsy on an infant was unbelievably disturbing. Many infant deaths were homicides due to an adult's selfishness and lack of paternal supervision.

In the summer of 1999, after almost a year on the job and hundreds of autopsies, there was an unusual invasion of homicides in the post room. Women of diverse races and ages were discovered rolled in carpet or found in dumpsters or abandoned fields and houses, most of them beaten, stabbed, shot multiple times, or burned. Their reports read that they were known to be prostitutes or runaways.

I had a lot of those cases, and they all had a story. I completed rape kits, swabbing their mouths and inside and outside of their genitalia, and I did pubic hair pulls or combs. Fingernail clipping was challenging because the fingernail clippers were covered in old blood, hair, and fingernails; that's cross-contamination. Watching the photographer take pictures of their faces, the battle scars, and injuries, I could see their pain. They were victims, girls to women, who had fought through their own trauma and grief until the end.

I thought about why the news didn't share these stories; there could've been a serial killer on the loose. "We don't want to create any type of mass panic. They're only prostitutes," said one of the investigators.

I was face-to-face with the gun violence victims the Judge had preached about five years prior. The number of homicides occurring in Detroit involving young African American males increased daily and they were overwhelming on the weekends. Some African American women and children died in the crossfire, or as some put it, they were in the wrong place at the wrong time. It was unreal. The inner-city black-on-black firearm homicides became more and more evolved.

"The gun violence has to be stopped!" I declared. I remembered my college classroom forum assignment calling to end gun violence. That weekend activated a clarion call to the horrific gun violence in the city.

That following Monday, I called the Judge.

"Hey, Judge, did you know that fifteen black men were killed by gun violence from Friday afternoon through sometime on Sunday?" I said, sobbing uncontrollably. I paused and then said, "And only four made the news."

"No, I didn't know or hear that," he answered with surprise. "I might have heard about one or two."

"I know, I know," I replied. "I checked the news too, but the tragedy wasn't shared with the public. You need to have your Handgun Intervention Program attendees come and visit the morgue for a *Scared Straight* kind of intervention on Saturdays." Something had to be done.

"Antoinette, I agree. You are absolutely right; the gun violence in the city is out of control," he agreed. "Who do I need to talk with to get this started?"

"Call the main office and ask for the administrator, and you'll be transferred to Mike. When you talk with him, let him know that I'm a former student and involved with your Handgun Intervention Program."

Birthed out of our conversations and advocacy to stop the violence and save black men's lives in Detroit, the Wayne County Medical Examiner's Office agreed to collaborate with the Judge. Within months, a partnership between the two was created for a *Scared Straight* kind of program called the Handgun Intervention Program known as HIP.

The Handgun Intervention Program was a court-based education program for defendants whose attendance at one four-hour session was ordered as a condition of their bond. At sentencing, the judge could also order defendants to attend additional sessions if he felt it would benefit them. The program targeted young African American men ages twelve to twenty-eight, who were first- or second-time offenders charged with carrying a concealed weapon and had no other serious charges pending. The program's goal was to prevent defendants from committing gun violence or becoming homicide victims themselves. The program stressed the importance of consequences, choices, responsibility, and nonviolence.

Saturday was the day to see the face of death. The Judge selected a handful of young people and older adults to join him at the Wayne County Morgue. On this particular Saturday, about a dozen bodies were laid on trays, their skulls cut and faces peeled, while other autopsy assistants removed brains and organs or sewed up the Y incision.

I worked on removing bullets from one of many cases—an African American male who was just twenty-three years old, shot multiple times over a pair of gym shoes. The Judge stood in the observation room, his brow wrinkled, and he looked very stern. I could hear his conversation with the group, talking about the consequences of violence. "This could be you lying on the table," he preached. "See, this gun-murdered victim looks like a lot of you—young, African American, and male. Carrying a gun will lead to one of three things: jail, life in a wheelchair, or here at the morgue—death."

On Saturday night, his voice was slurred, and I couldn't hear him very clearly. I think he'd had too many drinks. "You have to be the best woman I ever dated," he said. "You connected HIP to the morgue, adding that missing piece."

"I didn't do it; it was God who had me at the right place at the right time," I whispered. "That's what friends are for."

"Well, I appreciate you; you are exceptional."

"Special," I said sarcastically, trying not to say anything out of the way. "Thank you for appreciating me. By the way, I also have some slides of murdered gunshot victims that you can present to those who don't come to the morgue. Knight said you can have them."

Finally, I'd heard "appreciated," and that I'd done something right. Maybe he missed me too. If nothing else, it was no longer about him or me but how I could serve and help others.

"I'd like to have you as the community liaison for the Handgun Intervention Program," the Judge said. "And by invitation, I want you to take the program to Morehouse College in Atlanta, to inspire young, educated black men to save the lives of those who look just like them."

"Really?" I was beyond excited that I would be able to share my exposure and experience as an autopsy technician at Detroit's Wayne County Medical Examiner's Office and impact the African American community, hoping to save a life.

★ ★ ★

I had a unique ability to look at the body beyond its state. Though the corpse was dead for days or even hours, the eyes were the windows to the soul and stories untold. You could see the frozen horror and the fear as they knew they were next in line to meet the Grim Reaper. *CSI, X-Files,* or horror movies like *Friday the 13th* and *Saw* were no longer entertainment for me; it was my reality.

My exposure to death triggered an overprotective covering for my children and how I looked at the world and life. Some people are sick, the walking dead, their worlds cold and dark, and as an autopsy technician, I saw behind the scenes—the immoral and mangled corpses that would tell the stories.

I realized that life was related to death, the dash between them was our journey that connected the two. Their stories and how they died. May they rest in peace.

CHAPTER
12
LESSONS IN BLOOM

I n each of my daughters, I saw myself at different stages, even in their personalities, beauty, inquisitiveness, independence, behaviors, including social and familial withdrawal, sarcasm, and astuteness. Like me, they all had a little hustle in their flow. The game of Monopoly brought all of us together. They fought often, sometimes about stupid little things, but they'd always make up immediately afterward. I wanted to make sure they were very close, like best friends, having realized sisters are forever, but friends can change like the weather.

By this time in my life, my oldest daughter, Nicole, was fourteen years old and was a little more responsible than her sisters. She had more chores than the younger two, and I felt comfortable leaving the younger girls in her care when I wasn't home. I had my share of challenges raising Nicole, who often wished she was an only child. Like a contestant on *America's Next Top Model*, she was tall and slender, with an accented jaw and defined facial features. She had black, straight shoulder-length hair and full lips. She was a natural beauty who could rock any runway. I didn't make it through adolescence before becoming a mother, so I know it was a weird time for me to relate. I was living my adolescence from the outside, thanks to Nicole.

Although they were close in age, Nicole and Marie didn't share each other's clothes too often. Whenever Nicole would get new outfits, Marie became frustrated, as she felt that Nicole's hand-me-downs were her new wardrobe, for which she was resentful.

Nicknamed Brown Sugar, Marie felt neglected at times. In addition to her feelings about having to wear hand-me-down clothes, she was bullied as a kid about her crooked, gapped teeth, which made her self-conscious about her looks. Somehow, she was able to maintain a positive outlook, using her imagination. Drawing was her specialty. She loved creating stick people out of bread ties, playing with Fisher Price's little people, and reading was a favorite hobby. She asked questions about everything but was a great team player with her sisters.

Yvette was the youngest, eight years old, and the quietest of all three. She was bright, into books, and loved to play store with her sisters, counting money. "When I grow up, I want to work at the grocery store and handle the money," she would often say. Yvette hated clothes and shoes. As a child, she would throw her shoes out the window and streak through the house. She was the child who was given more breaks, and she was at an age where she was treated like a baby and told she wasn't old enough or responsible for going with her sisters or doing what they were doing. She got left behind often. I'm sure it sucked because she was left out of playing with the older kids, forcing her to hang out with me or share my time and space with Hassan or anyone I dated. She wasn't forced to be responsible like her older sisters, and her cute smile would get her out of a pickle, thus creating the brat.

As my daughters became young ladies, there was a gap in time during their teen years when I was overwhelmed by so many responsibilities—bills, co-parenting, working, and everything else in between. The stress often became a bit much for me. They labeled me paranoid, crazy, and a conspiracist. They might have joked about it with their dad, my family, or their friends.

I might have been a little overbearing, but when I look back in retrospect, I guess it was just my fear of them making the same mistakes I had made. Sadly, it blurred my ability to see that they weren't me. The fear itself, nevertheless, presented itself as a stumbling block. We'd talk about our day during dinner time, sharing stories about what happened in class and work. I shared some of my cases with my daughters and stressed the importance of safety and knowing your friends, enemies, even family. Maybe I was overprotective, but I didn't want my daughters to end up on a cold metal table with a toe tag as jewelry.

"In health class, we saw a video about birth; it was way scary. It looked painful and bloody, but it seemed to be more about after the kid is born than how to avoid having a baby," Nicole shared as Marie and Yvette snickered.

"Wow." I cleared my throat. "Well, I know that we haven't talked about that subject too much, but I want to make sure you know my rules and expectations for you, most importantly, any expectations for friends in your life, including boys. You want them to treat you with respect. Really, don't let anyone pressure you into anything you don't want to do, from drugs to sex. Having sex or doing drugs won't make you popular in the long run. And that goes for you too, Marie and Yvette," I added, pointing at them both.

"Yeah, yeah. Geesh, Mom, I got it. No need to say anymore."

"One of my cases was a teenage girl who had lied to her mother about going to spend the night at her girlfriend's. She ended up dead in the dumpster the next day, raped and stabbed to death by a man she'd met online on Myspace." So much for family discussion. It ended quietly.

During dinner with my girls or my mom and sister, I shared the crazy stories from the post room to cure their curiosity, especially when it came to the local news stories. They would watch the local news stories about tragic deaths and ask me questions like, "Did you get that one?" "What happened?" and "Did the news tell the whole story?"

I allowed my feelings, frustrations, and fears to get the best of me. My emotions were everywhere. Life's issues, challenges, and realities rushed in like a flood; I was overwhelmed. As babies, when they needed feeding, they cried with a waking cry, the only thing a baby could do. Then on to tweens, when they whined with piercing moans, sounding like cats fighting in an alley because they didn't want to go to bed or share their space.

In a thunderous voice, I screamed, "Just *shut up*, or I'm going to beat you with this belt! God, help me!"

I yelled, fussed loudly, and demanded perfection in school and at home. "I want all A's and B's, nothing less; when you get a C, it's concerning in my eyes." Keeping their room clean and organized was a priority; clutter wasn't an option. There were moments when I punished then unnecessarily for little things, from a lost mitten to spilled milk.

"Mama. Mama!" Nicole's horrifying screams proclaimed she'd seen shadows in the dark. "Can you leave on the light?" she whispered after we searched under the bed, closets, and behind the door.

"Just close your eyes; count sheep. Be a big girl and go to sleep."

All this built up into a cacophony of clanging symbols in my head as I felt my brain expanding to a breaking point. I was having a meltdown; I was lost in time and space.

My emotional turbulence when it came to relationships was reflected by the number of men I dated simultaneously. I had a date every day of the week, and I had others to provide whatever I needed. They fixed my brakes and the washer machine and paid my bills. But only one man was my buddy, Hassan. He was the only one who could quench my thirst like a cold glass of lemonade on a hot summer day. His lips' taste was succulent like a cherry Jolly Rancher; his scent was like aromatherapy. But he was also my storm. Issues from our beginnings were still very present. We had continuous arguments about my style of dress and my way of thinking things through. I'd go on the fly and figure things out, doing things my way.

* * *

In the next several months, the number of dead bodies at the morgue was more than we could handle, especially those from gun violence. After discovering the number of homicides that occurred the night before, we had a staff shortage because my coworkers called to check first as a deciding factor for coming into work. Also, there was the shortage of needed cleaning supplies such as soap, bleach, and the lack of space to store the dead bodies, and our refrigerator and freezer were stacked full. Days at work became crazy.

I learned how to cope as an autopsy technician, and its full engagement in death, by compartmentalizing what I saw, securing it away and mixing church and cognac on ice. After seeing thousands of sudden, unexpected, or violent deaths, I came to the realization that life is but a vapor. I questioned our human existence. We are created spirit, soul, and body. I found it impossible not to think about the spiritual dimension.

What's all this about? Why am I here? I wanted the dash between the day I was born and the day I would die to be my purpose and story. Finding my way back to church, I attended Greater Grace Temple in Detroit. I asked God to give me answers about the next thing for me to do and provide my daughters with a spiritual foundation. While on the road to spiritual recovery, I thought about settling down with someone I was sure my family would like.

He grew up in the same denomination, Apostolic, and that was a gold medal for me. At least that was what I thought. His name was Andrew. He was an attractive minister, light skinned, muscular, the same height as me, with a chiseled jaw. His brown eyes sparkled, complementing his boyish grin. He was smart. He was employed with a full-time career as an engineer for a major automotive company, and he didn't have any children. He and I dated for several months. For the first time, there was no pressure for sex.

He's the one! I thought to myself. *Job security, Christian, no baby mama drama, and he didn't ask for any ass! Yes, he's the one!* What more could I ask for?

Was it too soon? I introduced him to my girls, family, and a few friends, and I met his mother via the telephone. Andrew told me his mother was a prophetess, telling people their futures. Prophetess Caroline was her name. She seemed welcoming by her tone, and she called me daughter while worrying about who was going to take care of her now since her oldest son was going to be gone. That should have been a clue as to who I was dating, but I couldn't see the forest for the trees.

Andrew had his own place, which looked a mess, with clothes everywhere, dishes piled in the sink, and it smelled like corn chips. He kept his car in a similar fashion.

"Excuse the mess. When you work fourteen-hour days like I do, there's no time to clean up," Andrew apologized as he picked up empty cans and chip bags from the floor.

Andrew was the oldest of three brothers and a martial artist and yoga trainer. The bells should have gone off from how he kept his apartment and car and what he practiced. He was a man who studied a Hindu spiritual and ascetic discipline while professing to be a Christian. How could one practice a lifestyle consisting of two different worlds and religions? You must pick one, right? It's like oil and water—they don't mix. I should have asked a lot of questions, but I didn't.

Not too long after we started dating, he surprised me with where he wanted to take the relationship. "Antoinette, we've been dating six months, and I think you're the one. Will you marry me?" Andrew asked on bended knee as my daughters giggled in the background.

"Yes, I will," I immediately answered. Was I ready for marriage again? Was Andrew the one? What about Hassan? So many questions ran through my mind, but as far as I was concerned, a good opportunity was in front of me. For some reason, I still felt I could right all my wrongs with a new job, a new relationship, a new chance … anything new.

I didn't hesitate to call my mother to share the good news.

"Finally, a man of God," my mother said happily. She figured it was just what I needed, a good ole church man, somebody to help me get on the right path.

"Yes, finally, Mom. I think he's the one."

"Let's plan for my daughter a wedding!" my mom said. I could hear it in her voice; she was happy for me … happy for us.

As excited as I was, I couldn't help but think about the devastating news I had to deliver to Hassan. That evening, I called him and asked him to come over. I thought it would be better to tell him in person as opposed to over the phone. Of course, Hassan thought it was going to be one of those nights that turned into wild, kinky sex. But before he could get comfortable on the sofa, I broke the news to him.

"We can't see each other anymore," I said. My voice cracked. "I'm getting married."

"Getting married to who? What about us? What about me?" Hassan asked, obviously shocked by what had just come out of my mouth.

I was in no mood to talk. *We're like oil and water. It will never work.* I tried to convince myself of these things.

That night, I lost my best friend.

*   *   *

Months passed, premarital counseling was completed, and the wedding date and details were set. We chose Crystal Gardens for the ceremony. The reception was secured; my dress was picked out, and bridesmaids and groomsmen were selected.

I guess we were ready … but was I ready?

"Andrew, let's purchase a home before we get married." In my mind, it made sense to buy a home together; isn't that what couples do?

"I can move in with you, and we'll look for a house after we get married," he promised.

Just like that, I was at another crossroad in life, scared about making such a life-changing decision, especially when red flags were popping up left and right. For example, I don't think my mother-in-law ever saw me as a strong woman, rather a needy one who just *needed* a man. In the days leading up to the wedding, she began to take over all plans and their execution. I knew then that I was marrying the wrong man and marrying into the wrong family. But it was too late; the invitations were out, money was spent, and, most importantly, I had the opportunity to make my mother proud of me, so I had no other choice but to go along with the program … something I knew I'd regret as soon as I said, "I do."

★ ★ ★

A late-night storm uprooted trees, downed power lines, and broke the windows of various houses and buildings in the area. The weather was hot and humid, and with no air conditioning, I sweated my hair out before the ceremony began, leaving my once-bouncy curls shriveled up and almost unrecognizable.

"Maybe God's trying to tell you something," Carlitos teased, laughing uncontrollably.

"It's not funny," I snapped as I ran past him into the bathroom. I glanced at myself as I rushed past the bathroom mirror and into the stall. I was officially sporting an Afro. As I pulled my underwear down to use the bathroom, I was met with yet another unexpected problem—my period had started. The tears began to stream down my face like Niagara Falls. I had been meticulous with planning the wedding around my cycle. I mean, what bride doesn't take that into account? Since Andrew and I never had sex, I was especially looking

130

forward to our wedding night, when we could freely consummate our marriage.

After I'd gotten myself together, I washed my hands, straightened up my dress, and walked out of the bathroom into the hallway. Like a stoic robot, I let Marjorie touch up my hair and makeup and rejoined the wedding party ... only to go through with marrying a man I didn't know, didn't love, and didn't want to marry.

Not only did we not have sex that night; Andrew refused to even touch me in any sexual manner, stating some ancient Old Testament scripture about being "unclean." No need to tell you that things went downhill from there. I eventually discovered that we would never be on the same team. We would never be committed to helping each other as most couples do, and he never really assumed a stepfather role with my daughters. Essentially, our relationship-turned-marriage was on life support from day one.

We were divorced within six months. If I am honest with myself, I loved the idea of marriage but did not love the man.

★ ★ ★

I was highly recommended for a job at Career Works by a man by the name of Mr. Capeland. He was a club member at Fitness Works. I was hired on the spot by Career Works Inc. as a job developer for their Work First program. In the mornings, I'd have to drive across the city of Detroit, beating the pavement, knocking on doors, making phone calls to build relationships with employers, contacting businesses, from corporations to store fronts, and advocating for and pitching G.E.D classes. I did skills training and supportive services, such as day care, counseling, job referrals, transportation, and job fairs. In the afternoon, my role switched. I was responsible for providing hands-on skills training, helping clients prepare their résumés, doing mock interviews, and helping clients complete job applications. More than ninety percent of clients in my caseload were victims of domestic violence. I saw pieces of myself in many of these women. Had it not been for the incessant fight in me, I could have very well become one of those hopeless women.

I helped women dress for success. I saw women who were imprisoned, in rags, and living in poverty break the cycle of poverty with new attire that transformed their bleak realities into dreams come true. Their professional attire, be it an amazing two-piece suit, dress slacks, a blouse, a string of pearls with matching pumps, or a purse, was the tool to help them thrive in work and life. It was life changing. In fact, I helped Bernadette, who was between jobs. When she put on that Ann Klein suite and black patent leather shoes, she was ready to make a powerful impact during her interview. I saw my twin be empowered by dressing up; she was prepared for the world. Her confidence got her an entry-level job at Wayne County Community College. She climbed the ladder from answering phones in customer service to writing educational programs for the college's four campuses, continuing education department, and summer camps. I was proud to be a part of my identical twin's success, no longer a competition but a compliment to us as sisters. I was my sister's keeper.

As a single mother of three, I could relate, having walked a mile in their shoes. What a chance to serve in such a capacity. I went from serving people in health and wellness to discovering life through death, and now I was helping families escape poverty and be free of welfare slavery. I was trying to juggle it all by myself. That's when my Career Works family stepped in, those who provided help when I needed it most. The team helped me pick up my daughters from school, who, by the way, all went to different schools. Thus, this was no easy feat.

Career Works was like a big, extended family of sorts. We helped each other out. Lasting friendships were formed, and our children would grow up to become friends. We celebrated birthdays, sometimes even divorces, and we also comforted one another during tragic losses of loved ones. But no amount of acceptance from others could make up for the emptiness I felt inside. I felt as though I was a failure ... a complete failure. To my daughters. To my mother. To myself. It was these realizations that caused me to jump in my car one hot August afternoon and zoom down I-75 South and head to Chene Park. I felt lonely. Empty. Lost. Purposeless. The only constant in my life seemed to be pain.

I parked my car and walked over to the water. I could faintly hear the words, *"You'll never be nothing,"* ring so loudly as I stood looking out onto the Detroit River with the sun light glistening on the water. I closed my eyes, focusing on the sounds of the sailboats racing like go-carts on the water and the waves crashing against the rocks. As I stood, a warm wind captivated me. Something in the pit of my belly churned. And that's when I heard His voice say, *"Go back again and join the Detroit Police Department."*

Join the Detroit Police Department?

CHAPTER

13

WHATEVER IT TAKES

Have you ever wondered what it is really like to be a female cop? We look sexy in uniform, right? After going through months of preparation, physical and psychological tests, and background checks, and the most stressful of them all—the interview—joining the academy was finally upon me. I had made it. I was ready to protect, serve, and save the city.

It wasn't until I sat down that reality hit me, and I started to feel nervous about going into the Detroit Police Academy. I looked at my face, plain without makeup, free of coverup. Was I in over my head? Yes, since the day I'd moved my family into the city. But bravery would always arise. Becoming a police officer was part of my destiny.

Dressed in a khaki twill shirt and pants, I arrived at the academy at 7:15 AM on October 13, 2001. Big Jack had shown me how to iron military creases and shine my shoes like glass with a lighter to the polish and wrist power—back and forth with the shoe brush.

The classroom was packed. There were about thirty of us who reported to the academy that day. It was no longer a dream but a reality. Little did I know that the life I had known would never be the same.

My classmates were all ages, colors, shapes, and sizes. Some were former military personnel and others security guards, social workers, retail salespersons, or just fresh out of high school. However, one thing we all had in common was that we wanted to make a difference in society by way of becoming police officers with the notorious Detroit Police Department.

I was the oldest female in the group, which set me apart in a class by myself. In the academy, you learn what inspired your classmates to join the police department. I sat next to a young Caucasian woman who seemed to be in her upper twenties.

"What made you join?" I asked after I'd basically told her my whole life story.

"When I was in my teens, one of my cousins was murdered and her murderer was never found. I vowed I'd dedicate my life to putting away the bad guys. So here I am. What about you?"

Before I could answer, a loud voice rang out. "Get in line at the door." The directive was followed by yelling, screaming, and additional commands to get in formation in the hallway. I followed suit, of course. But it wouldn't take long before I stood out, not because of my eagerness to prove myself capable, but because of something else altogether different—my looks.

"You move, SPO?" Sergeant Williams roared, rushing my way.

"Sir, I'm fixing my tie," I nervously replied.

"You can't even manage to keep your tie straight. What else is crooked on your uniform? There will be no movement; we don't care if your nose itches. No one moves unless we tell you to!"

I swallowed hard as our eyes locked.

"Now get down and give me twenty push-ups, now," Sergeant Williams demanded.

Without hesitation, I dropped to my knees and then positioned myself. "One. Two. Three. Four. Five. Six. Seven. Eight ..." I collapsed on the floor, almost at the sergeant's feet.

"Give me fifty!" Sergeant Williams yelled to my classmate, Pierce.

Thank God Pierce finished it out. The antagonization didn't stop there. Sergeant Williams had it in for me.

"What are you looking at with those contacts and that Halley Berry haircut? You must think you're in Hollywood. Let me just remind you right here and right now, this ain't *Swordfish*. This ain't the movies. Everybody knows you have on colored contacts, and fancy hairstyles aren't worn in the academy. Why you wanna be a police officer?"

"I ... I want to save people, sir," I mustered.

"Sound like you need to be in church, doing altar call. And you look like you need to be sitting behind a desk as a teacher rather than being a cop and arresting criminals. Seems like you gotta lot of proving to do."

I did just that ... a lot of proving. That day, I proved I had what it took to get through the day. No amount of yelling, screaming, insults, or even physical challenges could make me quit. I had what it took to be a police officer, and I knew it.

* * *

After an exhausting first day of academy training, I learned that my roll call for my training for the next six months would be at 6:45 AM, not 7:45 AM. An hour earlier, which would cause a problem for me. How was I going to get three children to three different schools and be at work by 6:45 AM?

I ran through my rolodex that evening, but no one could assist, not my mother nor my sister and not even anyone from my Career Works family. I was desperate enough that I even asked Hassan. He couldn't help either. Frustrated and angry, I knew I had no alternative but to call JB, who by this time, was living his life with his new wife and their three daughters. It was his turn. I had done all I could in my power. Now, it was JB's turn. I pressed the seven digits and waited for JB to pick up.

"Hello," he answered in an unenthusiastic tone, having most likely, eyed his Caller ID and knew it was me calling.

"It's your turn," I blurted out without even thinking about extending a formal greeting.

"My turn for what?" JB asked, confused.

"Your turn to take the girls."

"Whoa ... wait. What are you talking about, Ann?"

"I don't have any help watching the girls while I go to work, and I need to do this for me and for them."

"Do you need me to help pay for someone to watch them?" JB countered.

"JB, are you listening to me? It's not just about someone watching them. I can't do this by myself anymore. I need you to take them," I said without taking a breath between words.

"Like in permanently?"

"Yes, like take them into your house with you and your new family," I said, throwing a little shade.

"Well, you know I have a house full over here. What am I supposed to do about room for them?"

"You and your new wife gonna have to figure that out," I shot back. "Since you've been remarried, you've been living like we don't even matter. You're taking care of you and your wife's daughters. Just add our three daughters and be the man in their life."

"Would you calm down!" JB said, trying to lower the temperature of the conversation.

"Don't tell me to calm down!" I screamed.

"I can't just do that. I have to talk to my wife first. You know how it goes."

"Well, you can talk to her before we get there!" I yelled as I pressed End on my cell phone, abruptly ending the call.

I sped down the interstate as though I was in the INDY 500. Out of the rearview mirror, I glanced at my girls, who were all sitting in the backseat with terrified looks on their faces. I'd forced them to pack a few things to last them for a week and promised that I'd pack up the rest and bring it to them later. The move was a big one, and they had no time to process what was going on. All they knew was they were going to have to stay at their dad and new stepmother's house. Although I felt horrible on the inside about the suddenness of the decision, I felt it would be better for them, especially for Nicole, who was exhibiting daddy issues. I reasoned within, *At least they'll be in a two-parent home with their sisters and a better school district than Detroit, which is more than I can offer.* And I found solace in that line of reasoning.

I parked in the driveway of the house JB shared with his second wife and her girls. He was my girls' biological father too. In my mind, they had every right to have their dad one hundred percent of the time.

"Come on," I said to the girls as I opened the car door and headed to the trunk to retrieve their bags. JB must've been looking

out of the window, waiting for us because the front door swung open
before we could even ascend the front steps.

"I told you that you couldn't just drop them off like this! There's
all kinds of preparation that needs to be made before you can just
move three additional people in your house. You and I haven't even
made arrangements on when you're going to take them."

"Well, too bad," I said as I began to walk up the steps. "When
the three new people are your own flesh and blood, you just do what
you gotta do. Like I did!"

"JB, what's going on?" a voice uttered from behind JB. It was
Shawn, JB's wife, who was holding their youngest daughter. She was
wearing a silverish-gold snake-print halter bikini top and matching bottoms. JB's blonde, hip-grazing-braids-wearing wife, Shawn,
thought she looked like Mary J. Blige. But she was far from it. In
her mind she was fine. She had a nice figure, perfectly carved cheek-
bones, thick, curly eyelashes, and a set of glittering white teeth. But
her wicked ways made her look wickedly beautiful in my eyes. In
other words, she was pretty on the outside but ugly on the inside. I
was blinded by the diamond ring; it shined like the morning sun-
rises. *JB didn't buy me a rock like the one she's wearing. But like they
say, "All that glitters isn't gold."* And I was certain that, soon enough,
she would come to realize that it wasn't about the bling-bling she
wore; it was about JB's children … hers and mine. And because she
refused to acknowledge the notion previously, she was being forced
to on this night and without warning.

Suddenly, I felt a surge of heat creep up my spine. She had some
nerve living in a mini-mansion and expecting JB to ration his love,
time, and resources to my girls. I was a human volcano, only moments from eruption, which was dangerous.

Recognizing the familiar stance, JB positioned his body in front of Shawn. "Nothing. I got it," he said.

I didn't wait for her to comment. I blurted out, "I'll tell you what's going on. JB's daughters are coming to live with y'all; that's what's going on!" I dropped two of the bags at JB's feet.

"You can't just do that!" Shawn yelled, moving around JB.

"Watch me!" I shot back. I turned to my girls and reiterated what I'd told them before we left the house. "You all will be living with your dad until I finish the police academy. Mommy will be back for you," I said with tears now cascading down my cheeks.

JB stood frozen, almost in the same spot he was in when he swung the door open. He was stuck between a rock and a hard place. He had five women to please, and he couldn't please them all. If you want to say the majority won, then the majority won—my girls were staying, and I was leaving.

Saying goodbye, even though I knew it was only temporary, was difficult. As I turned to give my girls a final goodbye kiss, Shawn yelled out, "Bitch! You're just a fucking whore wearing a uniform. I hope you get AIDS and die!"

I chose to ignore her comment, even though I was tempted to draw my weapon and dare her to repeat her words. But I knew that my girls had already experienced enough trauma in a two-hour window, so I bit the bullet and decided against that route and, instead, gave Shawn a verbal lash. "You are just jealous. You wish you could be me, baby. But I've been there and done that. Enjoy the leftovers," I said as I sashayed to my car.

As I got back in my car, a sense of relief and overwhelming grief overcame me at the same time. I was free on one end, but I knew that thought of not being a good mother was going to torment me. I'd made the most painful decision in my life. I did it for them; I

did it for us, and I did it for me. This decision was my only option. I'd considered what was in their best interest.

That night, I cried myself to sleep. That is, after several hours of tossing and turning, wondering what my girls were doing. At some point, I had to reason with myself. I had to be honest with myself. JB was more stable than I was. He could offer them what I couldn't at the time. I had always wanted my daughters to experience the childhood that my parents had given me—a two-parent household. I wanted them to be involved in extracurricular activities like track, soccer, basketball, and academic programs, go to church regularly, make new friends, live in a safe environment, have overall feelings of security, and most of all, have a stable parent. I knew that as much as I tried, I could not give them stability. Instead, I gave them a mother who acted like a teenager. I showed them how to not react when angry. I showed them how to not keep it together. But I was determined to show them how to make it and be living proof that dreams do come true.

I went from having them ninety percent of the time to a mere ten percent of the time. While they used to live at home Monday through Friday, they now only visit on some weekends. I knew that making this decision would mean sacrificing ninety percent of their childhood. I knew that I would miss out on conversations over dinner. I'd even miss Tuesday-night homework sessions and tending to Wednesday-morning tummy aches. I'd miss track meets and basketball games. Only for a short time. It wouldn't always be like this. One day, I knew they'd be back home with me.

* * *

"You will be called nigger, white boy, bitch, muthafucka, and even some names you never heard before. It doesn't matter. It is

141

nothing personal," Sergeant Williams said, his voice raised nearly two octaves. "To civilians, you're just a uniform and a star. So, if any of you all are sensitive types, you'd better get rid of that sensitivity or drop out right now," he continued as he walked down the rows, scanning each of us standing in formation.

The law enforcement code of ethics was an oath, the tablets and scrolls of police officers to uphold the law regardless of the race or social status of the offender. We were to eat, dream the code, and shit it out every day and at any given time.

Tact sergeants and officers in charge during roll calls, defensive training, and throughout classroom sessions all shared with us very insightful tips.

Number one: It's not what they call you; it's what you answer to.

Number two: Don't eat where you shit. In other words, we were strongly discouraged from becoming romantically involved with coworkers. Basically, you don't want to put yourself in a stressed situation by dating another officer, which could get crazy or ("shitty") at the precinct where you work ("where you eat").

Number three: It's not what happened; it's what you articulate on paper that is the key. These were the instructions when it came to report writing. In other words, if it wasn't documented, it didn't happen. We were told that there are three sides to the story—his, hers, and the truth—and as a police officer, a clear, concise, and detailed report was an absolute must. It determined someone's freedom or incarceration.

Number four: Keep it to yourself. In other words, if you do anything that you don't want someone else to know, do it by yourself and keep it between you and God.

Number five: Don't second guess yourself. Trust your first mind, which is your God mind.

Going against any of the code of ethics could be big trouble. These codes of ethics were our safeguards and protection. As a rookie, I tried my best to adhere to them. I wanted to do things right, move up in the force, prove myself to myself and others, and ultimately, get my daughters back.

* * *

In the months that followed, the training was accelerated, covering criminal law, criminal procedure, crime scene processes, investigations, and police tactics.

The physical training and conditioning were intense, requiring us to complete obstacle courses as well as never-ending runs, all of which were timed events. We also had weight training, weekly meal planning, defense tactics, and we worked through replicated crime scene enactments. Needless to say, it was through sweat and tears that I learned to eat less Hostess doughnuts and embrace fruit as a snack.

Firearms training was nothing like the movies; we had to learn about the 9mm Glock, how it works, how to use it, and how to clean the firearm. After classroom training, we trekked a long walk into a concrete pit, each of us carrying our paper targets to the gun range for firing practice. I was a nervous wreck; I had never shot a gun before.

"Center mass is the goal," yelled the gun range instructor.

"Hold it like a hard cock in your hand," whispered another gun range instructor, who was so close I could feel the warmth from her breath like a summer breeze.

I froze. *Is she hitting on me?* I wondered. I felt violated.

The targets were timed to turn at intervals and distances, a basic combat-shooting course designed to teach us how to fire rapidly at a moving target with accuracy. Being instructed to kill the bad guy dead in his tracks was disturbing, initially. But it was the firearms training at the gun range that began to change me. I felt my self-esteem rise. I began to feel more confident in myself and my abilities.

My luck got even better when I ran into the officer who offered to give me private firearms training. I could feel his eyes following me as I packed up my weapon. Finally, I turned my head in his direction. He smiled. I assumed it was safe for me to smile back, so I did.

"Getting the hang of it, aren't you?" he said, revealing his chipped front tooth through his smile.

Blushing, I replied, "I think so ... I think so."

"You are. I've been watching you," he admitted, giving himself permission to walk toward me.

"Oh, really?"

"Really. I mean, really ... I've been watching you, and you're getting better and better. With a little more practice, I would say you could improve your target accuracy by fifty percent or more and rise to the top of your class for High Firearms."

I can beat Young, I thought to myself. "You think so? That much?"

"Of course. If you have the right trainer."

"Guess I need to find a trainer," I said, zipping up my duffle bag.

"You're looking at one," he said, picking up my duffle bag before I had the chance to do so.

My mind immediately recalled the rules in the code of ethics class, and as if he could read my mind, he said, "Purely business. It's not the same thing."

"So, you're an instructor?" I said, pointing in the direction of the Exit sign.

"One of the best," he boasted.

Eager to do my best and be the best, I wanted to start right away. "When can I start?" I asked.

"Just say the word," he said.

"What about next Sunday?"

"Next Sunday is a go for me," he said. "And by the way, my name is Tracy, also known as Officer Tracy Wilkins," he added, extending his right hand.

"Antoinette Bostic, also known as Bostic," I said, extending mine.

He walked me to my car, and we exchanged telephone numbers before departing.

We chatted several times that week before our official training day the following Sunday. I skipped breakfast that morning and headed straight for the range for my nine o'clock training session with Officer Tracy.

"Good morning," Officer Tracy said as I entered the area he had reserved for us.

"I'm not late, am I?" I said, scanning the clock on the wall.

"No. No, you're not late; I'm just early. Been practicing, myself."

I watched as he wrapped up his target practice, admiring his targeting skills and accuracy. He was already at a place I wanted to be.

To say that he worked my tail off during our first session would have been an understatement. He was precise and skilled, pushing me beyond thresholds unimaginable.

"What are you getting into now?" Officer Tracy asked as he gathered his weapons and other artillery.

"I'm starving. Gonna grab lunch."

"I'll join you," he said, inviting himself.

That's how Officer Tracy and I began.

As they say, hindsight is 20/20. There was no book or training that would prepare me for what I was about to experience after graduating from the Detroit Police Academy.

CHAPTER

14

WOMEN MAKE GOOD COPS

I was ready, equipped, and prepared to save the city! The time had finally arrived. I would be standing in front of my three daughters, my family, and my friends, swearing to "serve the community; to safeguard lives and property; to protect the innocent against deception, the weak against oppression or intimidation and the peaceful against violence or disorder, and to respect the constitutional rights of all to liberty, equality, and justice."

With a new mayor and a new chief whose slogan was "Mind'n Our Business" as advertised on buttons that were mandated to be worn with our uniform, I would be birthed into a new family called law enforcement—the Blue Brotherhood. On that day, April 10, 2002, I was sworn in as a Detroit police officer during a ceremony held in the Wayne County Community College auditorium.

What a great time to graduate! The year I became a Detroit police officer, Kwame Kilpatrick became Detroit's youngest mayor. We both were African American and thirty-one years of age. How ironic was that?

I expected a world where the good guys won. Truth was considered an asset, but a good heart and pretty face would get a woman far. As an officer for the Detroit Police Department, I was dressed in a blue uniform with crisp military creases, with my black tie in place as my "A. Bostic" nametag, badge number 3641, and ink pen glistened in the sun. My thick leather gun belt was heavy, as it holstered my department-issued 9mm Glock, two magazine clips, and handcuffs snapped in tightly. I stood proud and tall. I had achieved one of my greatest dreams.

But underneath all the uniform and gear, I was literally smothering. The bulletproof vest fit more like an overly padded sports bra; I could barely breathe. *If I ever get shot below my breast, it will be the end for me!* I thought to myself.

Lights. Camera. Action! I was no longer watching cops shows from the screen; I was the main character, all the way live and in living color.

* * *

A police officer's life is filled with pain and joy, danger, and tragedy. But make no mistake about it, sprinkled in there from time to time is a little bit of humor. There was never a dull moment on the job. The moment you stepped into the station, you could hear ringing telephones, yelling voices, slamming doors, intercoms, news radios, and much more. *Hill Street Blues* had nothing on the Detroit police. And while the department, its precincts and units, were a culture within itself, each had its own practices, traditions, and subcultures, a secret language—a code of silence that extended beyond the lips of the police officers.

On one of my very first patrol runs, we had to respond to a call for shots fired. When we arrived at the location, we found a man lying in the street. I stood as close as I could without compromising the crime scene, just in time to see him take his last breath. At that moment, I was reminded of my days working at the coroner's office. I knew what was to follow for the victim, how he'd be laid on the metal slate and sliced open in an attempt to unveil the details of his death. Now, I was on the other side, no longer primarily focused on finding out why but finding out who. This go around, I didn't have to make calls to the family; I'd wait for the medical examiner to perform a thorough autopsy, and then turn over the information to be included in the police investigation, and later for evidence at trial. It was amazing to discover how the same information could be used in different ways, and both perspectives were equally exciting.

My first assignment out of the academy was in the Third Precinct. I reported to the Third Precinct in Southwest Detroit, which was known for its Mexican culture, from the people to the food and the art. Many of the residents spoke Spanish. When I walked through the doors of the precinct, I stepped into *Hill Street Blues*. The busyness of the station was inescapable—ringing telephones, conversations between police and citizens at the large front desk, scurrying traffic of officers coming in and out of the station and walking back and forth as they carried out their job responsibilities. I stood mesmerized as I waited to get my official orders. But before I'd have that such luck, I was introduced to one of my fellow officers.

"Welcome to the family. We don't see race or sex; we only see blue," one of the older white officers working at the desk said. I guess that was his way of greeting me.

I smiled and reached out my hand.

"Your assigned field training officer is off today, so you'll be paired with Officer Munso," the officer continued, pointing to the short Hispanic officer standing to my left.

"You look like Barbie in a police uniform," he teased, referring to my crisp blue uniform and spit-shined shoes.

"Look like Barbie, huh?" I said before pausing. I wanted to get a jab in, so I went for it. "So I guess it's Barbie and Papa Smurf today?" Officer Munso's smile faded. I knew I was a minority on the force, being black and a woman, but I'd be damned before I'd be reduced to the likes of a plastic white doll, not when I had worked hard through blood, sweat, tears, and selfless sacrifices. I had rightfully earned my badge and gun.

I spotted smirks on the faces of the nearby officers, who at this time, began to look away or attend to whatever they were doing before I put Munso in his place. Trying to minimize the blow to his ego, Munso changed the subject altogether. "Are you ready to go?"

"Ready when you are," I said, prepared to follow my so-called partner for the day.

I followed Munso to our scout car out back. Before getting in, I flipped the backseat and searched underneath the seats as well as the trunk.

"What's that for, Bostic?" Munso asked as I got in the car, having completed my task.

In the academy, we were trained to always search our assigned scout car before and after each shift, you know, to check for any weapons or drugs. "It's called CYA, cover your ass. Don't you remember?"

"I've been on these streets for about sixteen years and survived Desert Storm. CYA is different in the precincts and streets. Throw that academy shit out the window. Out here, you've got to be the *real* police," Munso teased as he started the cruiser and put the shift into gear.

The morning sun painted a gold splash of light on Mexican Town as children walked to school and commuters headed out in rush hour. Munso and I rode through the streets in our scout car, taking in the colors and architecture of the houses and buildings, the budding flowers, and the afternoon blue skies. The fresh smell of tortillas filled the air. The scenery made it seem more like Tijuana or Cozumel as opposed to Detroit. As soon as we turned off Michigan Avenue onto West Avenue, the scenery changed. It was like day and night. There were abandoned, charred, dilapidated houses and broken-down cars on the streets and in the driveways. Homeless black men wearing torn, dirty clothes walked the streets, pushing grocery carts, carrying "Will Work for Food" signs while frail-looking women dotted the corners, barley dressed and with uncombed hair. It seemed as though I was riding through a war-torn Middle Eastern country.

"Days are the best detail," Munso said as he zoomed in on a potential target, interrupting my daze.

"What?" I said, focusing my attention on the street scenery.

"All brass wants you to do is get a couple of tickets. And it's a bonus if you get an arrest with a weapon or drugs. If a suspect is wanted for murder, then it's a purple heart and a picture with the chief. You see, when we see an African American male walking on the street, wearing a backpack, black hoodie, jeans, and Timberland boots, it's the perfect target."

"Is that right?" I said, now looking at Munso with some measure of disbelief. It was difficult for me to fathom that police drove around in pursuit of a young black male target as a prize.

"Yes, indeed," Munso said, nodding. "Now, your ticket," he said, grinning.

"What are we stopping this guy for? Doesn't look like he was doing anything illegal to me," I said.

Without responding, Munso sped up. He flashed his lights and turned on the car sirens as he pulled up behind the "suspect."

I grabbed my cover and followed Munso as he jumped out to approach the young male.

"Hand ups," Munso demanded as he drew his weapon and unclipped his handcuffs.

Nervously, the subject complied.

"You got any weapons?!" Munso asked as he used his weight to separate the young man's legs.

"No ... no, sir," the young man answered with slight agitation in his voice.

"Get down," Munso ordered after he cuffed and patted the young man down.

"What's the problem?" the young man asked, confused.

"Uh, you were walking back there in the middle of the road where there's a sidewalk," Munso said, now standing over the help-less guy.

"I didn't walk in the middle of the road," the young man defended. "If you look on the sidewalk, there's an obstacle with debris in the way."

"I'm gonna need your ID," Munso said, feeling inside the young man's pocket for his wallet.

"For what?" he asked.

"Because I'm asking you for your license," Munso said, asserting his authority.

"I don't have a reason to show you my ID."

I stood on the sidelines, watching what was going on between the midget and the black giant.

"This is a lawful stop," said Munso, smirking.

"A lawful stop for what?" the perplexed young man asked.

At this point, I was confused too.

"For walking in the road where there's a sidewalk provided," answered Munso.

"There's debris on the sidewalk, and I walked around the debris. C'mon, I'll show you," said the young man

"No, no. That's great. I can see it from here," said Munso. I could see it too.

"You must be new, 'cause I ain't seen those eyes before," the young man said as he scanned me from head to toe.

I told myself that something wasn't right about this. He was on the sidewalk, not in the street. Munso grabbed the man's ID, tossed it to me, walked the young man to the scout car, and helped him get in the backseat.

"Run his name; he might have warrants," Munso directed as he closed the back door and sat in the driver's seat of the squad car. Unzipping the backpack as if he knew he'd struck gold, Munso searched through the young man's backpack. When he didn't find anything, he sucked his teeth and said, "Write the ticket for impeding traffic. It's just a violation. A misdemeanor citation, not a felony."

As I handed Munso the ticket, he smirked. Before I could even guess his next move, he got out of the car, ordered the young man out of the back seat, and uncuffed him. "Have a nice day, young man."

"What about my backpack?" the young man asked.

"It's mine now," Munso said, his smirk widening.

Dumfounded, the young man stood there and didn't move. Munso got in the car, rolled down the driver's side window and threw the backpack out of it. Turning to me, he said, "Welcome to the real police" as a wide grin spread across his face.

As we sped off, I had to get it off my chest. "Munso …"

"What?" he said, turning his attention from the road to look at me.

"You know that young man didn't do anything, right?"

"You don't get it, do you?"

"Get what? He was just walking … minding his own business, it seemed."

"Look, I did the city a favor."

"How so?" I questioned, totally oblivious as to what he was suggesting.

"By protecting the citizens from the likes of a criminal who'd dare step into the street for a minute to walk around debris that was blocking the sidewalk."

I didn't respond. I could tell that I was in for a rude awakening. This was not going to be anything like the cop shows I grew up watching on television.

★ ★ ★

I drove home in a haze that afternoon, reflecting on what had transpired on my first day on the beat. When I got home, I lay on my bed, exhausted. I couldn't move. The events from the day kept playing in my head, from being referred to as Barbie to the stop and ticketing of the young, innocent male. Things were different for sure. I was no longer Toni at Fitness Works or the autopsy technician at the morgue, zipping black men into body bags, nor was I the case manager helping to empower black women to live their dreams; I was now the woman behind the badge—a member of the Detroit

Police Department. That was the moment I realized I wasn't in Kansas anymore. There was no right, no wrong, no black or white, just blue.

It didn't take me long to become acclimated to the culture or the climate. I was relatively comfortable patrolling the southwest area of Detroit, which included the New Center area, Midtown, Corktown, around Wayne State University, and to the borders of the Canada bridge. After about six months, I was switched from days to evening, and I had a new field training officer, also known as an FTO.

Southwest Detroit was on the map for Mexican Town, where authentic Mexican cuisine was the best. A man by the name of "Crimson" was my FTO. We got along well. I liked our vibe. Up until this day, I thought I had done a good job of maintaining a low profile in the department. Apparently, I was wrong. As I went to retrieve our scout car that afternoon, I noticed a pink envelope tucked under the windshield wiper. Without touching the envelope, I examined its exterior. It was addressed to me. The words "Officer Antoinette Bostic" were written in bold font. I hurriedly unlocked the scout car, lay my belongings on the front seat, and grabbed the envelope. I opened the envelope to find a card with a cartoon drawing of a tiger that read:

> *You and I are apart. But I'm not going to be sentimental about it. As much as I miss you, I'll just have to make a mature adult adjustment to it.*

The inside of the card read:

> *Like the moon in the sky and the waves in the tide, know your love brings us back around no matter where*

I go. Understand this—I'll return in your life and you'll be mine. The love we shared. (Remember this, my sweet; I will be with you, even if time goes slow.)

XO
Always

I raced into the garage in a panic, showing Crimson and the sergeant on the desk. "Someone is stalking me," I said, fighting back tears.

"Someone has a crush on Bostic, leaving cards on the windshield," the sergeant on the desk said, laughing with Crimson joining him.

"Well, I actually think the card is kind of cute," Crimson said, taking the card out of my hand.

"This isn't funny," I yelled.

"Look, just relax, and stop acting like you're on the school playground."

I didn't respond. I knew from that moment that there was more to come, and the culture on the force was one that deemed incidents like this normal.

"Bostic, let's hit the streets," Crimson yelled.

Without further comment, I followed Crimson out of the station to our scout car. We were on what was known as the witching hour, patrolling the street, looking for drug deals, prostitution interactions, and the like. Peak hours were midnight to four o'clock in the morning. According to statutory code, prostitution is the self-indulgent exchange of sex favors for money or gifts. Most prostitutes were, of course, females serving male customers. Prostitution was prevalent in Southwest Detroit, from the strip clubs that lined

Michigan Avenue to the truck stops that were just minutes from the border of Canada on West Fort and Cass Corridor. The prostitutes' ages ranged from thirteen to sixty years old. Many of the women looked aged by drugs and diseases and who knows the number of johns they'd sold themselves to over the course of the years. Johns usually got away with buying sex on the streets until the blow job went wrong. That is when they would get robbed with a knife or by gunpoint, prompting a call to authorities.

We were on the beat in the southwest part of the city when we received a run: "person with a weapon," a person carrying a weapon at Silvers, a strip club on Michigan Avenue. According to dispatch, the 911 caller stated that an unnamed suspect was outside of the club firing shots with a black handgun. The description of the suspect was not atypical for the area—black male, light complexion, six feet, two-hundred pounds, black hair, beard, wearing a Pistons shirt, jeans, and Pistons cap. The Pistons were hot; Detroit had the Bad Boys on the court and the streets.

With lights flashing and sirens blasting, we headed for the strip club. Driving up, we didn't see anyone outside, so we proceeded to go inside the club. It was my first time ever being in a strip club. But it was like a scene right out of *Dancing at the Blue Iguana*, with dark blue lights, a smoky bar filled with drooling men and women eyeing thong-wearing, bra-less girls twisting and grinding on a pole as money was thrown at them. To my surprise, I wasn't shocked in a disgusted way. I was shocked in a different manner. The women were all beautiful. They came in all colors, shapes, and sizes, all wearing slinky lingerie in different styles, meticulously accessorized with rhinestone earrings and boots with matching rhinestones. I stood back and watched them dance seductively, bumping and grinding in an orgasmic rhythm to the music for the patrons at the booths; they were shining like diamonds.

Even though we were in full uniform and armed to the tee, the party never stopped. The women who were not on the stage appeared to be friendly, some even introducing themselves. I could overhear one of the dancer's introduce herself.

"How is everyone doing? My name is Strawberry. Would any of you gentlemen be interested in a private dance?" She was sociable, intelligent, and very pretty. Her brown eyes and smile sparkled in the dark. She had beautiful brown skin, smooth as silk, and her shape was like something out of *Playboy*. Time stood still for a moment.

"Bostic, snap out of it," Crimson said, realizing I was in a trance. "We need to get the manager's name, so we can go back to the station and complete the report."

"Okay." There were just as many bouncers as there were dancers, so I asked one of them to point me to the club manager.

"He's over there," the short, stocky bouncer said, pointing to a figure standing at the back of the club.

As we headed in the direction where the bouncer pointed, I could see him clearly—black male, light complexion, six feet, two hundred pounds, black hair, beard, wearing a Pistons shirt, jeans, and a Pistons cap. Bingo! There was our suspect.

I picked up my pace to try to get Crimson's attention. "Hey," I said, tugging on his arm.

"Yeah," Crimson said, taking his attention from the women dancing on the stage, looking at me.

"That guy," I said, pointing to the suspect.

"What about him?"

"He fits the description of the suspect."

"You're right, Bostic. But the rules are different here. Just get his name and let's call a pull-on paper and head back to the station."

I did as I was directed. But still confused, I voiced my concern after we left the club. "Why didn't we approach the manager? He was our suspect."

Crimson chuckled. "You don't get it, do you?"

"Get what?"

"When it comes to strip clubs and bars, we don't do much of an investigation unless there's a shooting or homicide. So if you ever happen to approach a scene at a strip club or bar and you see anyone blue, or a public prominent official, look the other way. You got it?"

"I got it," I said, confirming the indirect and unwritten order. In that instant, the hairs on my neck began to rise.

That night, I learned something else new—that's how it went. Certain people in high positions were protected.

As I lay in bed that night, all I could think of was the events that unfolded while on the beat for the night shift, especially the women at the strip club, and one woman in particular—Strawberry. I could see her eyes, her lips as she spoke and her strut as she glided around the club. There was something about her that I just couldn't get out of my mind. Who was she? Why did I feel an attraction toward her? I mean, I wasn't a lesbian … or was I?

CHAPTER

15

IT'S A FAMILY AFFAIR

"We take care of ours!" That's what the commander of the Eleventh Precinct promised as he firmly shook my hand, welcoming me aboard his ship. Patrol on the eastside was on a different level, the culture had changed from the diversity I had grown accustomed to in the Third Precinct and Vice to predominantly African American, with a touch of Muong and Indian.

I was excited to see more female officers at this precinct. Some worked different shifts, but it was good to see other women, which gave me some sense of reassurance. I no longer felt alone. Class 2002-D had each other's backs.

Strip Clubs lined 8 Mile, and when lit up at night, you'd think you were in Las Vegas. My transfer placed me on the four o'clock in the afternoon until midnight shift. On this shift, my partner and I responded more to after-school fights, shootings, armed robberies, and disturbances, which flooded dispatch.

"It's the two of us," Officer Sommore, my new partner, said with a smile after we swept our scout car for any weapons, drugs, or trash that could be forgotten or planted by another supervisor. I hopped in the driver's seat of the patrol car and we were on our way—the "Thelma and Louise" of that particular shift. We both had less than three years on the force but were determined to make a name for ourselves. Little did I know, I'd make a name for myself in ways unknown at the time.

Cruising through our area, Officer Sommore and I had a chance for some girl talk. We were both single mothers raising our children, similar ages, I had all girls while she had a daughter and son. But it was good to discover that another female officer could relate to me on so many of life's issues.

Within minutes, a red four-door Pontiac swept past us at high speed, blowing through a stop sign. I turned on the flashing lights and turned the sirens on.

"License and registration," I announced as I approached the driver's side window.

"For what?" the young male driver asked in a seemingly cocky manner.

"You're not gonna make this difficult, are you?" I said.

"You don't know who you're messing with," the young male shot back as he scrambled through his wallet and glove compartment to retrieve the requested items.

I sat in the cruiser while waiting for his information to run through the system. Clean … no warrants.

"Just write the ticket and let's get outta here. We need to go after some big fish," Officer Sommore said, looking through the side mirror. As she'd confessed earlier, she could hardly wait for our shift to be over, so she could go home and get ready for her hot date with her man. She never mentioned his name but shared that he was a civilian, someone she'd met on a police run, when he was carjacked and needed a ride to the station. How fortunate that Sommore did not have to deal with the high school dating scene and political rhetoric in the precinct.

It was a good thing we made no bets on receiving praise due to the amount of tickets we wrote that day, because we would have lost money. We were met with fury.

"Who the fuck do you think you are, patrolling the streets, making traffic stops like you're the police?! You just got off probation, which means you're still a rookie. Do you think you can write anyone tickets in my precinct?"

"No, Commander," I replied.

"Didn't they teach you anything in the academy?"

"Yes, Commander," I answered.

"Then what in the hell gives you the right to give out tickets for running stop signs to family?"

"I thought I was the police, Commander," I said, asserting my authority.

"The police?" So you writing the deputy chief's son a ticket? You think you're the boss?"

"No, Commander."

The Commander smirked. "Another pretty face but no brains. They don't teach the rookies nothing, like back in the day. Where's the ticket, Bostic?"

I handed him the ticket and watched him rip it into pieces right in my face, right before telling us to recover our things from the scout car and bring him the tape recording. So, doing as we were told, Officer Sommore and I retrieved our belongings from the scout car and brought the tape recording to the commander's office.

"Thank you. You won't be needing this," he said, snatching

the tape from my hand. "Now, enjoy the rest of your day," he said, opening his office door for us to leave.

I waited until we got to the locker room before I said anything. I was in tears, fighting to breathe. "He gets that kind of attitude about the deputy chief's son? What kind of commander is he? Like I'm supposed to know whose family is who and believe someone who tells me their mama is the deputy chief."

"It's about family, blue family and beyond," she replied.

There it was, application of the blue code of ethics. I was beginning to learn, albeit the hard way, that there was not just a blue code of silence but a loud horn that warned that when it came to the police department or police force, whichever term you used to describe it, the term "family protection" was broad, but its definition was clear. Essentially, everyone, including pets, were to receive special treatment. The letter of the law did not apply. Family members, especially immediate family members, were considered untouchables. Your job, your duty, was not to uphold the law at all times, but it was to protect "the family" at all costs. Although the lessons were tough, I wasn't ready to walk away from the force. I still had some fight in me. And besides, I was making good money and was nearly ready to have my girls back at home with me. So, what this essentially meant was that I had to go along with the program … temporarily.

Feeling a bit defeated that day, I decided to stop by the strip club. I couldn't get her eyes … her smile … her gaze … out of my head ever since I'd seen her a few months ago. It seemed as though we knew one another in another life somewhere. It seemed strange in theory, but in reality, it wasn't. We had a weird connection, but it was a connection, nonetheless.

Her Tommy Girl perfume lured me to her location, even without me laying eyes on her. I remembered the scent. There she stood, off to the side of the stage as the other girls danced seductively for the harem of men seated around the stage, frothing at the mouth. She took on the role of more of a mother or caretaker of sort, scanning the audience, looking to see who might be targeting one of the girls. Then, our eyes met. I waved at her, and she returned a half-cracked smile. Perhaps she was unsure of my motive. But since I was not in uniform, I felt confident that I could approach her without scaring her off.

As I walked in her direction, I could see her eyes scanning the room, looking to see if perhaps I was there as part of a sting of sorts. I wanted to reach out to her … touch her and let her know that she didn't have anything to worry about because I would not betray her. It was the first thing I let her know when I finally walked up on her.

"Don't worry. I'm off." I whispered, leaning into her ear.

"Good to know," she said, trying to speak over the music and screams of the club patrons.

I nodded, and for the next few moments, we stood side by side, pretending to be engaged in the dancing women on the stage, all while sneaking peeks at one another. She was still as stunning as I remembered.

I was pretty sure she said, "Let's go into the back" as she pointed to the back area.

I nodded, so she led, and I followed. We stopped in front of a small water fountain that was adjacent to the dressing room, where other half-naked women strolled back and forth, eagerly or nervously awaiting their turn to be called to the stage to show off what Mother Nature had blessed them with.

She took me by surprise when she asked, "No uniform today?"

I chuckled. "Oh, nope … not on duty today. I came for pleasure," I said, hoping she bought my sincerity.

"Guess I shouldn't be surprised," she said, returning a chuckle of her own.

"What do you mean by that?" I asked, wanting her to provide an explanation.

"Happens all the time. They come in for business one day and the next, for pleasure. Guess they like what they see," she said, winking.

I didn't want to admit to her that my first "official business" visit was also my first time being inside a strip club. She'd think she could get over on me. After all, I didn't know her, was just attracted to her for some strange reason. Strange because I'd never thought of myself as a lesbian, a "dyke," "butch," or "lesbo," as were the derogatory nicknames.

"I'll be getting off soon. Wanna hang out later?" she invited.

Hang out? I thought. *Where?* "Sure … I guess so," I said.

I took a seat in the main area and enjoyed the show along with the rest of the club patrons. That is until a man wearing a nametag with the name Patrick on it tapped me on my shoulder. "Strawberry said she's ready."

I grabbed my purse and followed Patrick to the back of the club. Strawberry had changed clothes. She was now wearing a pair of denim jeans and a cream and black hoodie. She was no longer wearing a full face of makeup. Actually, she barely wore any, just eyeliner and lip gloss. Even without makeup, she was still drop-dead gorgeous.

"I'm about to call a cab," she said, lighting up a cigarette.

"I drove. I can take you home if you want."

"That'd be nice," she said, smiling. "I'm safe, take a break and enjoy yourself. Tonight, I'm in good hands. I'm with a beautiful black female police officer," she told Patrick. He was her personal protection.

Did I just pick up a woman? I kept asking myself this question as we walked to my car, which was parked in an adjacent parking lot.

The drive to her house was filled with intermittent conversation, mostly about our backgrounds, which were similar. Like me, growing up, Strawberry had been raped … molested … you name it.

"That's why I don't give a fuck about the men who come to the strip joint. Bastards," she said, rolling down the window to toss out the gum she was chewing.

Unlike me, Strawberry wasn't religious. In fact, she was mad at God, sort of blamed him for allowing her to go through the trauma she'd endured. I didn't have any scriptures or words of encouragement for her. I was mentally tapped out myself. I had a rough childhood, a father who cared more about his life and lifestyle than his own flesh and blood, a mother who pretended her children's pain didn't exist, daughters I could no longer emotionally care for, and a job that was sucking out the little life I had in me.

"Do you want to come up?" Strawberry said as I pulled up to her nice high-rise.

"It's late," I said, not wanting to intrude.

"Come on up. You don't have anywhere to be at three o'clock in the morning, do you?" she said, smiling.

She was right. I didn't have anywhere to be, and neither did I want to go home. Home meant being alone, and alone meant confronting the demons that haunted me both day and night.

I parked in the lower-level garage and we took the elevator up to the main lobby. An older gentleman she called Mr. Ray greeted her with a warm smile.

"Good morning, Miss Beautiful," he said as he sipped on a hot cup of something.

"Morning, Mr. Ray. But you know it's really night for me."

"Yeah, you're right," he said, looking me up and down.

"My friend, Toni," Strawberry said, introducing but not introducing me.

"Nice to meet you, Toni," Mr. Ray said.

She pushed open the door to an immaculately kept condo. As I removed my shoes at the front door, my feet sank into the plush cream-colored carpet. Expensive artistry adorned the side walls in the front room, and a large flat-screen television hung on the center wall in front of the large gray sectional sofa.

"Your place is beautiful."

"Thank you. Most people are surprised when they come here. The taste doesn't quite match my trashy occupation."

"Well, I get it," I confessed. I mean, who was I to judge? If I didn't pursue my dream of becoming a police officer, I could have easily given in and done the same thing. I mean, I did have both the looks and the body.

"Anything to drink?" she offered, pulling off her hoodie.

"Water," I said, wanting to keep it safe. I had downed two drinks at the club already, and the last thing I needed was to catch a DUI. Going through the stalking dilemma on the job was more than enough drama for me, especially being a rookie.

"Ice?"

"Yes, lots of it." I always drank ice-cold water and loved eating the ice.

"I'm gonna change into something a little more comfortable first," she said as she disappeared into the back area of her condo.

I sat down on the far end of the sectional, admiring the

sophisticated décor in the room. A large hand-drawn color portrait of a little girl sat on the credenza cabinet below the large TV. With long ponytails, the little girl looked to be about five or six years old. Next to the picture of the little girl was a picture of Strawberry receiving what looked like her high school diploma. For a moment, I wondered what had transpired in her life that took her from a graduation stage to the strip club stage. From holding her hand out to receive a certificate for her brains to holding her hand out to receive dollar bills for her beauty. We were no different. I just probably had a little more fight in me than she did.

My thoughts were interrupted when she stood in front of me in nothing but her bra and panties, holding a bottle of water in one hand and a glass of red wine in the other.

"Your water," she said, handing me the bottle of water.

"Thanks," I said, accepting it.

"You have a beautiful place," I complimented again as I loosened the bottle's top.

"Thank you," she said, sitting down next to me.

"Who's the little girl in the picture?" I said, pointing to the hand-drawn portrait.

Strawberry paused before gulping down her full glass of wine. "My … um … my um … daughter, Kacie. She passed away." A single tear escaped her left tear duct and slid down her left cheek.

"Oh, I'm sorry. I didn't mean to … to bring you back to—"

"No, don't be sorry," Strawberry said, interrupting me. "You didn't know."

I didn't want to ask another question about the portrait. Truthfully, I felt awkward. "Maybe I should leave," I said, feeling foolish for being so nosy.

"No, don't … don't leave," she begged, placing her left hand on my right thigh. "She died in an ice-skating accident. Well, not on a real ice-skating rink. She had this obsession with ice skating. I'd promised her I would take her ice skating, but I just never got around to it. Made every excuse to not take her. So, one day when I didn't have time for her, like I often didn't, I took her over to my parents'. She called herself ice skating on the pond in the backyard and slipped through a crack in the ice. The neighbors found her and called the paramedics ..." She paused.

"You don't have to finish. I can figure out what happened."

"They ... they couldn't save her," she said, now sobbing.

I took her wine glass out of her hand and placed it and my bottle of water on the coffee table in front of us. I leaned over and hugged her tight, caressing her back in circular movements with both of my hands. I felt her body relax as it went limp. The weight from her thin frame felt heavy against my chest, so I leaned backward, trying to position her weight off my torso. Her tears began to fall again. This time, in a steady flow, saturating my shirt as each one escaped her tear ducts, traveled down her cheek, and dropped onto my shirt. Gently lifting her head from my chest, I cupped her face in my hands. "It's gonna be okay. Kacie's in heaven. I'm going to help you get through this. I'm not going to leave you," I said, wiping the tears as they continually flowed.

"I believe you," Strawberry said, holding her head up with her own might.

Our eyes met in that moment, and our lips found each other's. The tenseness in my body began to dissipate. *No, Toni ... this is wrong.* This was what my mind kept rehearsing, but my heart gave my body—my hands, arms, eyes, lips, legs, and vagina—permission to explore every spot on her body. And the sentiment was mutual. Strawberry gave herself permission to do the same to me. This wasn't about lust; it was different, something inexplicable. Unnatural, as the church called it. But for some reason, it felt authentic. It felt right. Every touch, stroke, and thrust seemed to touch the deepest pains in my soul, each moan seemingly releasing some trauma from our respective pasts. But as much as it felt right, in a very tangible and spiritual way, I knew it couldn't ever be openly expressed by either one of us.

The next morning, our words were very few. Everything we needed to say to each other had been expressed the night before, right there on the gray sectional in the living room. Our uttered goodbyes were merely ritualistic in nature. We both knew we weren't finished with one another. We both still had some loving and healing to do … with each other.

*　*　*

I was moving fast on the force. Opportunity after opportunity was flowing my way. Although things weren't perfect, I was filled with a newfound hope and optimism. I walked into the station ready to hit the streets and save the world. But that hope was short lived because I was summoned to the commander's office upon my arrival at the precinct.

"Not again," I mumbled as I watched him reach into his drawer and retrieve an envelope that had been addressed to him. Even at a glance, I could discern that the handwriting on the envelope appeared as though a ten-year-old practicing cursive had written it.

"I received a letter, and Sergeant Cass did too," my sergeant said as he held the envelopes up in his right hand. "Read the letter addressed to me first. It's on the top," he said.

Butterflies danced in my belly as my sergeant leaned over and handed the letters to me. It wasn't over. As a matter of fact, it was probably just beginning. The setup to force me out, that is. My trembling hands clasped the envelopes. I paused a moment before carefully lifting the flap on the top envelope and retrieving the handwritten letter.

"Hey, Commander. You got to know P.O. Bostick is hoeish and bi-sexual. They say she is a cock-sucking trick who loves to lick clit. She get mutherfuckas to pay her. How you think she rollin' 'round in that Ford truck? She was fuckin' Dan over at Vice. That's how come he put her out. He could no longer keep his eye on her 'cause she get around. She freaking with that white hoe Molly on the shift. They both bi."

Without looking up at my commander, I opened the other envelope addressed to Sergeant Woodward and retrieved the letter from it:

Bostick is a freakin' bisexual. She licks ass and fucked your whole staff. Don't let that skinny-legged, no-tits freak fool you.

Suddenly, my vision became blurry. I could no longer read the contents of the defamation letter. I blinked a few times, and my vision came back into focus. I looked up at the commander. The look on his face was one of utter disgust. But shock was not one of my primary emotions. Although I didn't have a mirror, I was certain my face was beet red; I was embarrassed.

"Still no idea where these letters might be coming from?" he asked.

ANTOINETTE M. JAMES

"I have no idea who would want to do this to me."

"No, Bostic. Listen to what I said. I didn't ask you who. I asked you do you know where they might be coming from. There's a difference. In other words, have you done something to someone and they're trying to get you back? Seeing a married man?"

"Whoa, Commander. You're asking me about my private life, and it has nothing to do with my job," I said in my defense.

"Oh, but it does. When you put on that uniform and that badge, you automatically become a target. And for the record, there's no such thing as private life. Everything, and I mean everything, is the public and the force's business. That means your spouse, your children, your parents, and your pets too."

"Well, I don't know where this is coming from, and neither do I know who it's coming from," I replied as my mind raced through my black book of dates, trying to figure out which guy had the potential character to do something like this.

"Can I give you a piece of advice?"

I nodded.

"Watch yourself and be safe out there," he cautioned.

"Can I have a copy of the letters?" I asked.

His eyebrows raised. "You sure?"

"Yes, I'd like to keep a copy for my records," I replied. Yes, I wanted a copy for my records, but I was also concerned about the letters suddenly vanishing and then reappearing at some other inappropriate time to varnish my reputation or be used as ammunition to force me out. I made two copies of each and handed them back to my commander.

★　★　★

172

"Someone's out to get me," I said to Sommore in a somber tone as we headed out that afternoon.

"Out to get you, how?" she said with a quizzical look.

"Somebody mailed the commander a letter, saying that I was a hoe, bisexual, fucking for money and my truck, and even screwing Molly. That's some crazy shit!" I yelled as I pounded my fist on the dashboard.

"What! Who do you think it is, Toni"?

"I don't know," I whispered. *Big girls don't cry ... big girls who are cops really don't cry. We control our emotions,* I convinced myself as I tried to shake feelings of victimhood and helplessness off. It was time to fight crime, and I couldn't appear weak in any form or fashion.

By the end of my shift that evening, my mind was already at the strip club, although my body had to catch up. I grabbed a bite to eat on the way home from work and sped home afterward. I had a couple of hours to spare before heading to the strip club to see Strawberry and the girls perform. It was becoming ritualistic, a pattern I couldn't seem to break and one that I didn't want to break either. There was something enticing, alluring about my relationship with Strawberry, also known as "Alana." On stage, she was eye candy for sex-thirsty men and women, a sexual being for our pleasure, but offstage, she was Alana, a lost soul in search of her innocence, which had been stolen, snatched up first by a fifty-six-year-old pervert she affectionately called "Granddad." In like manner, my onstage performance, so to speak, came in the form of a uniformed police officer employed by the Detroit Police Department. But my offstage persona was just as lost and traumatized as Strawberry's. Although she'd lost her daughter in the physical realm, I'd lost mine in the emotional realm. We were two battered souls, trying to heal each other's equally battered souls—a plight that was too great for both of us.

CHAPTER

16

THIN LINE BETWEEN
BLUE AND HATE

I grew up watching *Columbo*. I thought the show was super exciting. Columbo, the chief investigator, had unique mannerisms
and an unsophisticated charm that allowed him to solve the
most difficult crimes. I loved watching the entire series. As a kid, I
had an insatiable desire to be a homicide detective. Watching *Hill
Street Blues*, reading *Nancy Drew* and *The Hardy Boys* stories, and
my training as an autopsy technician at the Wayne County Medical
Examiner's Office had all prepared me for this new opportunity.

On December 1, 2003, I began evidence technician training,
known as crime scene investigation, or CSI. It was a three-week,
five-day, eight-hour accelerated course. Training took place on the
southwest side of Detroit. Our trainee group was made up of ten
officers. We were different ages, sexes, and races.

Preparation for this line of work was to train our minds to vi-
sualize the undetectable, to see the missing piece to the puzzles, to
connect the dots so to speak. Sometimes, the answer to the question

is in the details. And I'd take many of the principles I learned in the academy and apply them to my personal life. As I'd later learn, when I didn't, I learned lessons the hard way.

Police Academy Rule #2: Don't eat where you shit.

I had the dating blues. From lyrics to films, I'd heard it all—that love would keep relationships together; when it came to love, think like a man; and love was like a game; sometimes you win, and sometimes you lose.

Being a police officer, I would see it full circle, from the fractures and breaks to the hurt and death. Whether the relationship was heterosexual, homosexual, or anything in between, in each one, the common denominator was always a love that had gone wrong, a loyalty that had been compromised, or a trust that had become shattered. Once any of these occurred, all bets were off, and the results could be catastrophic.

But in my world, my motto was, "If they can do it; I can do it better!" when it came to dating relationships. My line of reasoning was that I wasn't going to be held to a double standard when it came to my interpersonal relationships. I had seen so many male officers make their rounds through the department, even dating women from other precincts, sometimes two and three women at the same time. It was a common practice, one that was taboo to talk about, even though everyone knew it was happening. Those in higher-up positions refused to deal with this behavior on the police force, partly because they were partakers in the behavior and practice themselves. So it went without question that someone—some person you may have dated—could literally grow angry or bitter and send letters and tapes to your place of employment to scandalize your name and have you viewed, not as a victim, but a perpetrator. This very notion fueled a different flame in me. I was determined to have total control over my personal life and date how I saw fit.

First dates, for me, weren't typical. I'd come with a set of questions, some of which included, *Does he have a criminal record? Is there a photo of him at the precinct for Most Wanted? Does he do drugs? Is he a drug dealer? Does he drink and drive? Is his license suspended? Is there baby mama drama?* And in some clever fashion, I'd find a way to ask these questions and get answers to them. So, whereas the average woman would try to find out whether a man had money or owned a car, I'd be trying to find out much more. I learned that many of my fellow female officers thought the same way. You see, we would wonder if he drove a hot car too. However, it meant something entirely different in our world. Since most of us could obtain the finer things in life, sooner or later, we weren't focused so much on materialism; we were more concerned about whether a guy was good in bed.

My male partners always seemed to have the best of both worlds, even those who were married. There didn't seem to be a shortage of women for them, and I noticed that there wasn't a shortage of men either. Some joked about having to decide whether to handcuff their love interest and take them to jail or take them home for a night of S&M.

Women love men in uniform. The police uniform makes men seem ultra-masculine, confident, brave, and strong. Although women in the same uniform can have those same qualities, they weren't usually considered attractive qualities for a female. Wearing a nurse's uniform rather than a police officer's uniform was, however. Relationships for female cops were challenging. We were labeled "too serious" or expected to be into S&M because of our access or regular handling of handcuffs, batons, and a Glock. Some men even said that female officers tended to treat everyone like a suspect, always placing them under the microscope. Some of my challenges were obvious: I couldn't date criminals or brass, or my brothers in blue. Sometimes, however, they seemed to be the only people around, and there were plenty of them. I saw them as their fans and admirers did—masculine, commanding, courageous, and strong. Lucky for me, I had the pleasure of working side by side with them every day.

I decided to call Officer Tracy to pick his brain a little. I wanted to see if he'd gotten wind of what was going down at the precinct, as far as the stalking and harassment were concerned. I'd dated a few in blue, but it was always kept under wraps for the reasons I named previously.

Unexpectedly, Officer Tracy invited me to lunch, and we ended up at Sinbad's, a restaurant known for its delicious grilled salmon, one of my favorites.

I spotted a beautifully wrapped gift box on the table as the host was escorting me to the table where Officer Tracy sat.

"Hey, sorry I'm a little late," I said.

"No worries. Have a seat," he said as he slid the gift box across the table in my direction. "Here. This is yours. Open it."

I hesitated, not wanting to show anxiousness. I couldn't show him my cards, not yet. "In a second," I said, pretending that something on the menu caught my attention.

Officer Tracy sat patiently, watching me. I could see his every move out of my peripheral vision. Finally, I laid the menu down and carefully lifted the gift box. "What's in it?" I said, shaking it gently.

"Just open it," he said, smiling from ear to ear.

I meticulously unwrapped the gift box and retrieved a small black velvet jewelry case. Inside, I found a fourteen-carat-gold necklace with a gold cross hanging from the chain. "Oh my, Officer Tracy! This is absolutely beautiful."

"Thank you," he said. "But why are you still calling me Officer Tracy?" he said, chuckling.

"I dunno … guess I'm just used to it. I like it," I said, hunching my shoulders. I paused.

"What?" Officer Tracy said, trying to read my mind.

"What's this for?" I said.

"Just a token of my admiration for the work you do. I know it's hard being a female cop. You don't always get the praise or recognition you deserve."

He was right, and his verbal acknowledgment, in and of itself, was praise enough. I found myself fighting back tears. The last thing I wanted him to know was that I was moved by his words. I still had to play the tough game because, at the end of the day, he was a man … and they often came with heartbreak and other drama.

"Well, I truly wasn't expecting this," I said, closing the jewelry case and placing it back in the outer box.

"I don't know why we stopped dating—"

"Dating?" I said.

"That's not what we were doing?" he said quizzically.

"We were kicking it, remember?" I said, trying to refresh his memory. He told me on more than one occasion that he "liked kickin' it with me." Interpretably, he was letting me know that he had no intentions of getting into a commitment with me. I knew all too well what the phrase meant.

"Oh … that was then," he said, trying to act as though things would be different for this go round.

I liked Officer Tracy, but he had left a bad taste in my mouth, and I wasn't going to make it easy for him … if I decided to give him another chance.

"So why don't we just do this ... start over. Would you like to do that? This way, we both start off on a clean slate."

I chuckled. "Does that mean no more baby mama drama?" I said, reminding him again that the reason we stopped "kickin' it" was because of him, not me.

"No more drama. I got that under wraps now," he promised.

"Okay. We'll see. Let's take it one day at a time."

"Want something to drink, a glass of wine?"

"Just a Coke, ice on the side."

"Oh, I forgot you love Coke."

"Yes, Coke, baby, any day and any time," I said, winking.

"Now, remind me. What are your goals on the police department and where do you see yourself in five years?" he asked.

"I still want to be a homicide detective. It's been my dream since I was a child," I happily replied. "I've already completed evidence tech training, and I'm number eight on the waiting list," I added.

"Seems like you have a plan. Remember, if you need anything, don't hesitate to ask. I've got years under my belt and plenty of connections."

"Thanks, I will," I said as I tried to flag the waitress so we could order our drinks, his glass of red wine and my Coke.

"You seem like you like the outdoors. Do you?"

"I sure do," I said as I picked up the menu once again and began to peruse it.

"Maybe we can go white-water rafting or hiking one day," he suggested.

"Thanks, but I'd rather go to the beach," I said, smiling.

We ended up enjoying a good meal together and sharing a few laughs, deeming this reconnection lunch a successful one. Essentially, we both viewed it as a greenlight to future dates, as Officer Tracy now called them. Apparently, he'd abandoned the term "kickin' it."

★   ★   ★

Wanting to spend more time with the girls, more so out of guilt for me, I spent the next couple of weekends with them. This is when I realized my girls were changing. My oldest daughter, Nicole, was noticeably distant and always carried a bad attitude. When I confronted her about it one day, all hell almost broke out in my house.

"Ma, can I go hang out for a while?"

"Hang out? Where?" I said, looking away from my cell phone.

"With some friends," Nicole said in a snooty tone.

"Excuse me?" I said, throwing my phone down on the sofa next to me.

"Friends. With some friends," she said, trying to correct her tone.

"Well, I thought the purpose of you guys coming over was so we could spend time together."

"Me too. But seems like you can't get enough of your little boyfriend calling back-to-back. If I didn't know any better, I—"

"All right, Nicole! That's enough!" I said, standing up.

"That's all you ever do when we come over … talk to your men. You act like we're not even here."

"We just came in from the mall, Nicole. I bought you everything you wanted."

"You sure about that?" she said, putting her hands on her hips.

I paused. I knew she was hinting at something else. I looked into her eyes, and that's when I saw it … emptiness. She was turning into the teen I used to be when my world was spinning out of control.

Fighting back tears, I reached down for my phone and walked to my room, giving us both space we needed in that moment.

I walked into my room and closed the door behind me. Leaning against it, I thought about the trauma I endured in my teens. Guilt engulfed me. I knew then that if I didn't hurry up and find a place to live where we could all be together again, I was going to lose my girls. Emotionally, that is. JB might have loved the girls, but his wife surely didn't; she was barely tolerating their existence in their home. The words "evil" and "stepmom" go together as smoothly as ice cream and hot fudge. Hats off to Disney movies. Whenever a Disney flick needs a supervillain, it appears as though they select a woman from somewhere in the heroine's life. For my girls, it was their father's new wife, and they had complained about her more than once.

I walked over to my bed and fell face down on it and began to weep uncontrollably.

★　★　★

"What's the matter? You've barely touched your food," Officer Tracy said, leaning over the restaurant table.

"My girls," I said, twirling my life in the pasta.

"What about them?" he said, now leaning back in his seat.

"I'm losing them, I think. They need me."

"Bostic … you're a cop. You have a demanding schedule. You work crazy hours and are never home. That may be worse. Plus, if they come home, that'll be the end of our … you know what."

"Are you suggesting that I abandon my girls just so you can spend the night at my house when you want?"

"Abandon? You did that the night you dumped them off on your ex-husband," Officer Tracy said, looking directly at me as he took a sip of his Coke.

"I'm gonna pretend that you didn't just say that," I said, dropping my fork. "And I'm ready to go now," I said, taking the napkin off my lap and throwing it on the table.

"I'm sorry, Bostic. Really, I am. I didn't mean for it to come out that way," he said, standing up.

"I'm ready to go now," I said as I strutted past him, leaving him at the table to pay for the food I didn't eat.

I kept my attention focused on the scenery as we drove from the restaurant. My feelings were hurt. Perhaps Officer Tracy was telling the truth—I had abandoned my girls. Without making it noticeable, I wiped a tear that had escaped my right tear duct and attempted to make its way down my cheek.

"I'm really sorry, Bostic. I didn't mean for it to come out the way it did. I really had something planned nice for us today. Will you let me make it up to you?"

I glanced over at him; his lips said sorry, and so did his eyes.

"So can we just go and enjoy the rest of the day I had planned for us?"

I nodded gently.

We drove to an area called Troy, Michigan, nearly an hour drive from where we both lived and worked. We were out in the boonies, as they would say. As Officer Tracy pulled into the parking lot, I looked up and read the sign. Embassy Suites. It didn't take a genius to know why he begged for forgiveness so hard. Up until this point, I'd managed to keep the relationship clean. No sex. But I was sexually attracted to him and didn't have any constant man in my life, which meant I was beyond due for sex.

I followed Officer Tracy to the room that he'd already checked into. The room had rose peddles from the door to the bed, with candlelight and Godiva chocolates, which weren't my favorite; I liked chocolate-covered raisins the best.

After a double round of passionate lovemaking, we both dozed off to sleep. When I woke up, Officer Tracy was still dead to the world. *Guess the sex was too much for him,* I thought. Leaning over, I reached into my work bag that I carried everywhere, even when I wasn't going to work. I pulled out the *Atlantic Monthly* October 2003 edition, which included an excellent expose on "The Dark Art of Interrogation: A survey of the landscape of Persuasion." As I flipped through the pages, Officer Tracy woke up.

"Hey, sleepyhead," I teased as I continued to peruse the publication.

"So, is this what I gotta look forward to when we get married?"

"What?" I said, looking at him.

"You fucking me and then going back to your work?"

I laughed. "You were sleep, boy," I teased.

"Hey, that's one thing I ain't … I ain't nobody's boy," he said, grabbing my arm.

"Let me go. I was just joking," I said, snatching my arm away. I threw the publication down on the bed, got out of it, and began to put my clothes on.

"Where are you going?" Officer Tracy said, sitting up.

"I'm assigned out next week for interrogation and interview training. And I also have an interview for the mayor's wife detail with the Executive Protection Unit, so I need to prepare for it."

"Oh, so you want to learn interview and questioning methods and techniques, plus work on the mayor's wife's detail?" he said in a condescending tone.

"Oh, you don't think I can handle it, do you? I'll show you," I said as I tucked my shirt in my jeans.

"Come back to bed," he said, patting the comforter.

"No, I'm not coming back to bed," I said, sliding my feet into my shoes.

"What's this?" he asked, picking up the publication.

"It's a magazine my mother gave me to help me study," I said, holding my hand out for him to hand me the publication.

"Who's Dr. Cayman?" he asked, scanning the subscriber label on the publication.

"What are you talking about?"

"You heard me. I said who the fuck is Dr. Cayman?"

I didn't answer. Officer Tracy was no dummy.

"Are you fucking him? Yeah, you probably fucking him and somebody on the mayor's staff too," he said, whirling the publication across the room.

"Have you lost your mind?!" I yelled. "He's my mother's fucking doctor, that's who he is, and she picked up the magazine while sitting in his office for an appointment!"

"Yeah, I met your kind before," he said, now getting out of bed too.

"Look, I don't have time for this. But I want you to know one thing. If I was fucking him, I wouldn't be here with you," I said as I walked toward the hotel room door.

"So you think it's okay to be with me and fucking someone else? You think I'm going for that shit?!"

"Tracy, would you calm the fuck down? That's not what I said. You're putting words in my mouth! I gotta go. Call me when you get yourself together," I said as I opened the door and walked out the room, leaving him there to wonder whether he'd ever see me on a non-work-related case.

★　★　★

Valentine's Day weekend was one I'll never forget. As I lay in my bed, I could hear the faint sound of an ambulance siren, which was shortly followed by blaring police sirens. I glanced over at my clock. It was two thirty in the morning.

Someone's in serious trouble … maybe a possible domestic call ending in violence, I pondered as I lay in the bed awake. Living in the New Center Area, just blocks away from Henry Ford Hospital, I experienced both the pleasure and pain of seeing and hearing emergency vehicles and police cars lights and sirens at various times throughout the day and night. The sirens always symbolized that life was in jeopardy. The victim was possibly minutes or seconds away from death.

At six thirty that morning, my phone rang. My body stiffened. Call it discernment or instinct, but I knew something was wrong. I reached over and answer the called.

"Bostic!" Kennedy yelled on the other end. "You need to get to Henry Ford Hospital! Everybody from class is here!"

"I'm on my way," I answered. Before I could inquire on what had transpired, Kennedy had already hung up.

I got ready in a flash, ran down more than ten flights of stairs from my penthouse apartment, and jumped in my car. Only a few blocks away from the hospital, my mind raced as I traveled down streets as the sunrise cracked the early morning stillness. I felt as though I was driving in slow motion. *Why is everybody from my academy class at the hospital? Who's hurt? A car accident or shooting?*

One thing was for sure, Kennedy's voice sounded alarming, and I knew whatever happened couldn't have been good.

I pulled up to the hospital and sat in my car for a few minutes. "This must be big," I said out loud as I observed police cars and news trucks and cameras everywhere, including CNN. *You must face whatever this is*, I told myself. I took a deep breath and got out of the car.

I was greeted by security, who made me wait for a few minutes before he answered the door. The hospital lobby was filled with men and women in blue.

"I'll take you to the waiting room," the security officer said with flat effect.

He escorted me to the elevator, and we went up to the fourth four. As I stepped off the elevator, I was greeted by thunderous conversations. There were even more officers circling the waiting room on the fourth floor, including the homicide division, who typically wore trench coats and alligator shoes. As I pushed my way through the crowd, I saw my classmates huddled in a corner, talking and hugging one another. No, it wasn't good.

I spotted Kennedy but was trying to see who was missing. He didn't speak at first; he just stared at me, hard and emotionless. I stared back, looking at him as squarely in the eye as I could. I tried to hold back my tears.

"It's Fettig. She and her partner where shot early this morning during a traffic stop. He died on the scene and she's on life support," he said as I approached him.

"Doesn't look good for her either?" I said, looking for clarification.

"No. They just wanna keep her on life support until her parents are flown in from up north."

I shook my head in disbelief. I couldn't believe what was

happening. We'd only been on the job for two years. My entire body felt numb. Maybe for the first time since I had been a cop, the reality of being killed in the line of duty hit me. We stayed at the hospital until most of us had to be somewhere else, be it home, at work, or at some other required place.

Twelve hours later, Fettig, my classmate whom I'd shared a locker with, succumbed to the injuries she sustained from the gunshot wounds. Something in me died too that day. But something in me also lit up. The mission to catch the officers' killers was our number one priority. The events surrounding the murder were blurry to begin with, and all we wanted was to get to the truth and put the killers behind bars ... for good.

I walked through the doors of the Wayne County Medical Examiner's Office, where the autopsies of Fettig and Bowen were being performed. In an eerie way, the autopsies would confirm, sign, and seal their fate. As I entered the post room, the noise of saws cutting and banging could be heard as the autopsies were underway. Homicide detectives observed the autopsies as well.

I swallowed hard as I viewed my classmate's body lying motionless on the metal autopsy table, with her head propped up on a plastic block marked only by a toe tag. There was so much life ahead of her; she had just moved into a new apartment, gotten engaged, was looking forward to working as a homicide detective with yours truly as her partner. But now that dream was dead, just like she was.

The more I tried to make sense of this tragedy, the more complicated it became. I tried to connect the dots of how a traffic stop to pick up a prostitute led to the death of my classmate and her partner's death. I felt and knew that things didn't add up, but I didn't have the proof. With the amount of corruption going on in Detroit, it would have been no surprise that information was purposely being covered up in the investigation into the officers' deaths.

Thousands gathered at Greater Grace Temple in Detroit to celebrate the lives of two fallen officers: Fettig and Bowen. Movement seemed as though it was occurring in slow motion. The voices of singers, clergy, and those rendering tributes were faint, as if they were far away. The church was filled beyond capacity with a sea of blue, more than six thousand police officers from nearby towns, out of the state, and family and friends who had all come to honor and pay their respects to two fallen heroes. "Officer Forty-Five down!"

As the funeral service came to an end, it began to pour down raining on the thousands of police officers who'd lined blocks of West 7 Mile. Bagpipes played as the bodies of my classmate and her partner were carried to the hearses. From the church to the cemetery, the funeral procession was miles long with police cars, sirens, and shining bright lights. You could even see your everyday citizens lined along the streets and freeways, many with saddened faces as if they'd lost a dear friend or relative as well. Many waved American flags as they watched the procession pass by.

It was in that moment that I recalled the words we'd learned in our Detroit Police Academy training. *Final Rule: Don't second guess yourself; it could be a matter of life and death for you or you and your partner. Trust your first mind, which is your God mind.*

In my mind's eye, I could also see Fettig's smile that first day of class. Now, instead of smiling at me, she'd be smiling down on me as my guardian angel.

CHAPTER

17

SPECIAL INVITATION

"O fficer Bostic you have been requested for an interview with the Executive Protection Unit for the mayor's wife. Be there tomorrow. You are scheduled to interview tomorrow with the wife." And that's all he said. Unexpectedly, I had been nominated for an assignment with the family of Mayor Kilpatrick, Detroit's youngest mayor, his wife, and their three sons.

I was instructed to bring my résumé and arrive at the Coleman A. Young Municipal Center the next day. I was greeted by the commander of the EPU when I arrived and then escorted to a small office just outside of the mayor's office.

As I sat waiting outside of his fishbowl office, the mayor and his female aid passed by. I would finally see them in person instead of just on the news. He was taller and larger than he appeared on TV, and his aid looked different too; she was thinner in person. The mayor's office was just as busy as the station, with people walking back and forth, seemingly engaged in important work. The only difference was at the station, they wore uniforms, but at the mayor's office, they wore suits.

Suddenly, I heard the loud voice of a woman talking about an interview and going to lunch before getting the kids. And there she was—Mrs. Carlita Kilpatrick, the mayor's wife. She was accompanied by a man and a woman. She offered a warm smile, which showcased her perfectly set of white teeth. We were introduced and I was escorted into the interview room.

"Do you have an extra copy of your résumé?"

"Sure," I said, retrieving my résumé from the folder I was holding.

She went into the whole "So tell me about yourself" saga. I was happy to tell her about me. Afterward, Mrs. Kilpatrick basically took control of the remainder of the interview. She informed me that she had three sons—a set of identical twins and a busy toddler—all who had very busy schedules, which included afterschool sports, tutoring, and other activities. Work would also include her own agenda, a laundry list of things, from planning the mayor's community events related to children and seniors, hair appointments, luncheons, and various meetings. She didn't hold back voicing her biggest concern, which was her family and my ability to serve in that capacity.

"So, you do know that this assignment won't be a walk in the park, don't you?"

"This is something that both you and I have in common. I have three daughters, and their safety is my biggest concern as well. I can assure you that if I'm selected for this assignment, you and your family's safety will be my number one priority. I will see to it that not a hair on your heads is harmed."

"That might be easier said than done," she said, peering over the rim of her eyeglasses.

"I'm up for the challenge," I promised.

With her constant nods and aha's, I could tell that she not only believed me but believed *in* me. At the end of the interview, Mrs. Kilpatrick shook my hand and welcomed me to the EPU team. My excitement was apparent as I walked out of the office, smiling.

The unit's commanding officer gave me a tour of the mayor's office. His office had amazing views of the Detroit River and Canada's picturesque skyline. The colorful carpet accented the cherrywood desk and bookshelves. It even included a one-chair barbershop.

From the mayor's office, I was driven to the infamous Manoogian Mansion, the home of the mayor, where I was given a tour. The mansion looked like something out of *Better Homes and Garden*. The four-bedroom, four-thousand-square-foot home had been beautifully and tactically remodeled. Large windows let in sunlight in every room that faced the Detroit River. The chef-style kitchen, with its dark cherrywood cabinets and stainless-steel appliances, was something to behold. The mansion even had a bowling alley in the basement. The outdoor landscaping outlined the backyard, which included a swimming pool and boathouse.

Following the tour of the mansion, Belle Isle was the next stop. As we approached the water fountain, a black scout car and red SUV pulled up. My former sergeant at the Detroit Police Academy stepped out of the SUV.

"Hey, Bostic," he said, welcoming me to the unit.

I was sure he was the one who had nominated me for the assignment. He told me from day one that he'd look out for me. But as much as he was happy for me, he was concerned about me as well.

"Bostic, I know you're excited about this assignment, but I want to caution you that the next level of training is extreme. It's executive protection training, or EPT, which includes an advanced training exercise that you must pass before officially starting with the Executive Protection Unit. Be ready."

* * *

I was thrown right into the fire. I met with the Special Response Team—Mailman, the Rock, Hulk, Spider Man, Green Lantern, Storm, Rain, Thunder, Black Lighting, and Magic, all code names for other members of the team who had specific duties and responsibilities. Each would teach me the principles and etiquette of executive protection, threat assessment, evacuation, and drills regarding ambush, advanced motorcade operations, vehicle down, vehicle change over drills, arrival/departure review, advanced details/preparation, self-defense, armed and unarmed defensive tactics, in addition to firearms training and tactical shooting. It was a lot to cover in just one week.

I was tested on everything I learned, passing each one with relative ease. The final test was for special response, a hands-on and intense simulated, real-time training, which I passed as well.

"Great job, Bostic! You made it! See you tomorrow for phase two!" Sergeant Love yelled out to me.

"Tomorrow … phase two?" I said, trying to catch my breath.

"Yep. Meet me at Belle Isle by the water fountain at eight AM, and don't be late."

I cracked a smile. On the inside, I was disappointed. Friday nights were usually when I'd treat myself to dinner at Flood's, enjoying some catfish, fries, and a drink. Then I'd top the evening off with a rendezvous with whomever was the lucky guy of the night. I was no longer seeing Strawberry much. Our little "thing" was fizzling.

But with the training on my plate for Saturday morning, I knew I wouldn't be able to enjoy any of the above desires.

"I won't be late."

*   *   *

I arrived fifteen minutes early to the mayor's office, making sure I wasn't late. I wasn't sure what I was getting into, but I knew I'd worked hard training for the assignment. There was no way I was going to let myself down, let alone the mayor or his wife.

I was able to get an up-close and personal look at what went on behind closed doors in the political arena. Appearing to be in a hurry, Mayor Kilpatrick grabbed his hat and coat. Before exiting, he introduced me to his chief of staff, Christine Beatty, and welcomed me to the team. Christine, a little unfriendly in demeanor, acknowledged me with a slight nod. Before we could engage further, the two of them rushed off, with the EPU team following closely.

*   *   *

The hard work was paying off. I found a new apartment in a high-rise luxury apartment, similar to the one Strawberry lived in. My girls were home with me. I couldn't have wanted anything more. Things weren't perfect; I still had issues with teen growing pains, but that was to be expected. We were together, and that was most important. But just when I thought there was consistency in my schedule, where I could enjoy spending time with my daughters, attending their school basketball leagues, chilling at home with them, and putting them to bed at night, I would experience another shift. My initial shift was from 8:30 AM to 5:30 PM, Monday through

Friday, but it fluctuated according to the mayor's family schedule, including weekends. From daycare, to school, and afterschool sport practices, be it basketball or gymnastics, political speaking engagements to Monster's Inc. on Ice at the Palace of Auburn Hills, to the Beyoncé concert at Joe Louis Arena, and the Youth Easter Egg Hunt at the mansion, I had to be there to protect and serve.

At no time did I believe my job would ever be easy. I was well aware of that. As with my personal life, my professional life consisted of ebbs and flows of good and evil. Although I was on a different assignment, the attacks on my character from an unnamed stalker continued.

I received a call from Sgt. Lee one Wednesday morning. "Bostic, Lieutenant wants to see you at the office. Take the unmarked car, so parking won't be an issue."

"Thanks for the love," I said as I grabbed the keys and dashed up the stairs of the station and out the door. The drive in seemed like it took an hour, even though it was only minutes. From the Castle to the Coleman A. Young Building, that is.

My stomach churned the entire time. I had a gut-wrenching feeling that whatever I was being summoned to the office for wasn't good, especially considering the ongoing investigations being conducted by the attorney general's office and the state police.

Smiling faces greeted me at the door. My palms were sweating, my head was pounding, and I swore I could hear the beat of my own heart. Somehow, however, I managed to greet them in like manner, offering a warm smile.

With each step, my heart beat harder and faster. When I reached the office door, I pushed it open.

"Good morning, Bostic. Come on in. Close the door and have a seat," my lieutenant said, looking up from the paper he was reading.

As directed, I closed the door and took a seat in front of his huge desk. I felt as though I had taken a seat in the electric chair and was waiting for the switch to be turned on.

"Good morning, Lieutenant," I said nervously.

"I received a letter and a cassette tape in the mail regarding you. Both were addressed to the sarg. I don't know who wrote it, but it was signed anonymous," he said as he handed me the letter.

I inhaled. Nope. It wasn't good. Another letter was one thing. But a cassette tape? *Of what? Of who?* I thought.

"I haven't listened to the tape, but I threw away the envelope. And by the way, the commander at the Eleventh Precinct has a letter too."

Letters and a tape!? What? Who? Where? When? Why? How? My mind was on a rollercoaster attempting to figure it all out as I sat there. I could feel anxiety overshadowing me; I was already launching my own investigation on who the culprit could be ... how I could set up my own sting ... how I could be vindicated.

Slowly, I opened the first letter and read its contents.

> "*Sgt, what up, man? Nobody must have checked out that new bitch named Bostick from the 11th Precinct. I ain't hatin', but she could be trouble. She tryin' to put on a slick front. She keeps a log on stuff. She's loose as all get out too. I know 10 niggas that done freaked her. They say anything goes with her. They say she like to clean and eat niggas' assholes out ... her tongue long as most guy's dicks. And she goes both ways too. She got a connection to a major drug dealer. She uses her pretty face to get what she wants. She think she better than people from Detroit. We hear her talk shit all the time.*

She was freakin Lt. Dan at Vice. They transferred her out cause he wanted to keep his eye on her. She is headstrong. She like to drink. Get a couple of Long Islands in her, and the freak is on. don't be fooled by that 3 daughters talk. She drops her young daughter at her twin sister's place and goes out freakin', and her other 2 daughters do they own thang. The truck she drives belongs to her ex-husband's wife, and the wife don't know it cause Bostick is still fuckin' him. Bostick's friend at 11th lives upstairs from Bostick, and she's jealous of Bostick cause Bostick be getting' with mutha-fuckas and she don't. She said Bostick gotta nigga or two that she fuck with in front of her daughters, but they don't know Bostick is a hoe. Like I say, Jefferson, I am not hatin'. She got friends at IA through that noble group. She in there givin' a party this Friday night at Westin Hotel for the chief.

By the time I finished reading the letter, my hands were shaking like leaves. Slowly, my eyes moved from the paper to looking at my lieutenant.

He took a deep breath before speaking. "Bostic, there's enough going on in this unit, with the news investigation about the party at the mansion, to the rumors about the mayor and his chief of staff having a thing going on, and everything else in between. We don't need any more attention. I called Commander at the Eleventh Precinct, but he doesn't want you there either," he huffed with disgust.

"Lieutenant, none of this is true," I said, holding up the letter. "None of it."

"Possibly, but that doesn't take the negative stain away."

"So … what are you saying?"

"I think you should go to the Domestic Violence Unit and Internal Affairs and file a report so they can start an investigation. And instead of going back to the Eleventh Precinct, Lieutenant Dan wants you back at Vice."

Demoted. Here I was, the victim of stalking by someone who was out to, not only destroy my career, but destroy me as well. I offered no counter idea. Instead, I politely left his office and raced up Woodward to the Domestic Violence Unit on Cass.

After signing in and completing some preliminary paperwork, I was assigned to an investigator by the name of Jamieson.

"So, how can I help you?" Investigator Jamieson said, looking up at me.

"Someone is mailing sexually explicit letters to my commander and sergeants at the Eleventh Precinct and now the sergeant at Executive Protection," I said as I handed him the letters. And even though I was the police, wearing the badge and carrying a gun, I was terrified and in fear for my life and my family's.

Investigator Jamieson recorded important details and intercepted the letters that I had, but what came out of his mouth could have knocked me for six.

"Just because you don't know who's stalking you or sending these types of letters doesn't mean there will be an investigation."

"Even with all the evidence I've just given you?"

"I wish it were that easy. But if you do get any calls, notify me immediately. Same with the letters. The more the better," he said matter-of-factly.

CHAPTER

18

THE EYES HAVE IT

*P*olice Academy Rule #1: It's not what they call you; it's what you answer to.

In my case, it was what they write about you that had me shaken. And I couldn't live in fear or be afraid, let alone speak of my own pain. How could I admit that I was hurting when I didn't know the enemy? As a police officer, I knew that being vulnerable would get you hurt or killed. So I shook it off, straightened my badge, repositioned my gun in its holster, and went back to work.

It was good to be back at Vice. I felt accepted. Working under-cover was the most thrilling assignment outside of being assigned out for evidence technician training. To work with the rock stars was enthralling and a privilege. Vice was a place where there was no masking the person behind the badge. Our crew was a talented team of law enforcement professionals who shared deep camaraderie, family issues, personal frustrations, issues in everyday life, and our hopes and dreams. A separation of powers didn't exist in Vice. Even our supervisors shared their woes with us.

Working undercover Vice, I adopted the role of a prostitute, role-playing and dressing up. Halle Berry had nothing on me. I had everything in my wardrobe to fit the set: white patent leather and leopard-print miniskirts, matching go-go boots and fishnet stockings. And the wigs … I had every style and color.

"Your wig is the same hair color as mine; somebody is going to think you're me!" my identical sister screamed and cried.

"You're overreacting! It's not that serious. I'm the police, and I've got you covered!" I yelled back.

"Being the police, I accepted, but going from working security for Mayor Kwame Kilpatrick's wife and kids to being an undercover prostitute, I cannot take! Not to mention, when I'm walking downtown for lunch at Fishbones to get some fried catfish or cheesecake or when I go to Harbor Town to grocery shop, everyone thinks I'm you, including your fellow officers and men at gas stations." She cringed. "I just want to be me, but everybody in Detroit thinks I'm the police and catch an attitude if I don't speak."

"Don't worry; I've got you covered," I repeated. "Remember, I'm the one with the badge and the gun, so you're protected. I'll be safe, and so will you, the girls, and your kids," I explained, trying to convince her that she had nothing to worry about.

"I fear for your safety and ours, with all the scandal going on about the Manoogian Mansion party. And you're working the streets, dressed as a hooker … You could be a target, and one day, you could be the prostitute who gets shot and killed; that could be your story."

My sister was right, but it wasn't my fault we were identical twins. I was living my dream mixed with a nightmare, like J. Lo's character in the movie *Angel Eyes*.

There I was, back at it. Doing decoy work. And while decoy

work was interesting, fun, and exciting, this time, I was different than before. The thought of who was out to get me was trying to take up all the space in my mind. The constant blues was almost too overwhelming, but I couldn't help it. No matter how much I tried to lift my head and walk with confidence, I was haunted by the embarrassing letters written about me, defaming my character, both personal and professional.

As I stood on the corner under decoy, the wind numbed my already cold skin. I couldn't feel anything, and I wondered what it was like to be dead. I wondered if it was just what I was truly unable to see ... or the reality of what I just refused to see. There was a difference. I mean, I used to think that this kind of shit happened in movies and on television, only to discover that it happened in real life even more. The truth of the matter is that real life stories are played out on the big screen to expose and unmask reality with a hint of fiction. I began to question why I ended up being routed back to decoy ... undercover. Was what was happening in my life part of my destiny, and my past experiences had just prepared me for it all?

Many of us on Vice were all about the same age but had different years on the job. Some couldn't see the bigger picture; they were blind and oblivious to it. Maybe they could see and just learned how to turn a blind eye to what was now crystal clear to me—the code of silence within the police force was permanent. It was impermeable and definite.

I had to buy an entire new wardrobe. But it was time, back to playing dress up, decoying as a prostitute. I walked the streets of Detroit; I owned the corners and arrested the johns seeking to pay for sex. The underground activity had its own unique culture, and it was in plain sight. Prostitution was a lifestyle for hundreds of women, teenaged girls, some men, teenaged boys, and transgenders.

Most prostitutes were homeless, bouncing from place to place. Very few of them had valid IDs. By this time, I had met hundreds of them—wasted ones, overweight ones, and a few visibly pregnant ones. Some were toothless, others walked around with open sores on their skin, and there were those who were covered with scars. Some admitted to reusing condoms or having diseases, while others shared stories of how they would shoot up heroin or smoke crack. *My God, what happened to them when they were young?* I thought to myself.

The settings where sexual activity took place were slum motels, vacant buildings, dirty apartments, weedy alleys, even the backseats of stripped-out stolen cars. Nevertheless, a sting operation was just that, a sting operation, and there was no room to think about the psychological trauma the prostitutes had been through in their lives, at least not in the moment. This was about crime, quotas, and arrests.

At about a quarter after midnight, I noticed a red two-door vehicle occupied by two people. The driver was a black male, and the passenger was a white female. My eyes connected with his. *On a scale from one to ten, how bad does he want it?* I asked myself. At that point, he stopped to let the female out of the car and made a U-turn toward me. He took the bait, and he was mine, my last catch of the night.

He stopped on John R at Winchester and rolled his passenger window down. "Get in," he said, confident that I was desperate enough for his money, no matter how much he was offering for "my services."

"What's up," I replied in my girlish voice.

"I want half and half. How much?" He was desperate; it was in his eyes.

"It's whatever. I'm just trying to feed my kids," I said.

He pulled off. He was pissed that I didn't hop in as he'd directed. I pulled out a cherry cigarette that I used for props and began to puff on it. I knew he'd be back. About a mile down the road, I could see his brake lights come on as he made another U-turn and headed back my way. I was ready for him once again.

"Twenty dollars," he yelled out the passenger window as he pulled up on the opposite side of the road.

Got him. I signaled for the takedown crew to approach. The takedown crew, which consisted of five backup officers, quickly intervened. They stopped the suspect's red two-door car.

My work didn't end there. There was always the formal report that had to be completed and submitted. And as I was wrapping up the report for the night's activities and arrests, my sergeant walked up to me.

"You caught a big fish tonight," he said with a grin.

"A big fish? What do you mean?"

"You got a big player," one of my fellow officers said, chiming in.

"A big player? Who is he?" I asked, totally oblivious to whom they were referring to.

"A pastor at one of the biggest churches in Detroit!" my sergeant said, almost ecstatically.

I arrest one of the biggest pastors in Detroit, and he doesn't look familiar? I thought to myself. Whether he was a big fish or a small fish, all I knew was that I was doing my job. He was out on the prowl, searching for some head and pussy and got caught. And just like any fish, he'd fry by suffering the consequences of his actions. But that rationale was further from the truth than I realized.

The next morning, Lieutenant Dan got a call from the brass, stating that Mayor Kilpatrick had placed a call to the police chief, directing us not to show up to court for the pastor's arraignment.

"Are you serious? Don't go to court so the judge can dismiss my case?" I said, fuming under my collar. There it was again, another coverup. Those in high places could do whatever they wanted and get away with it. But this time, I wasn't going to play the game. "I'll be at court. I'm not letting this case get dropped … not this easy.

My crew had my back. We ignored the brass, the chief, and the mayor, and appeared at the 36th District Court for the pastor's arraignment. We sat in the lobby, waiting until the case was called. I could hear loud cheering around the corner, the voices growing louder and louder. There he was, in a suit and tie, as if he were clean as a whistle. This time, I got a good look at him. He was short for a man. But his cockiness and boldness stood as substitutes for his height. I watched as he shook hands with everyone he passed and waved as though he was some king.

"Ready?" my sergeant asked, noticing that I hadn't taken my eyes off the pastor.

"I sure am," I said. I wanted him … the big fish, as they called him. He was too confident that his money and his connections would get him off. But it was those very things that made me more determined than ever to stick a fork in him.

"Just want to let you know, so there are no surprises, the mayor told me yesterday that this case is not going to go forward."

"Why not?" I challenged, now looking at my sergeant eye to eye.

"The pastor's lawyer requested the case be postponed."

"That's bullshit, Sarg, and you know it is!" I snapped.

"Look, if you know like me, you'll save yourself some time and energy. Let him go. He's got the money and the connections," my sergeant finally offered before heading out of the court.

It was difficult for me to accept this reality, but he was right. It didn't matter how many appearances we made at the 36th District Court on that ticket. Each time, there'd be a different judge, but the results would be the same—not guilty or scheduled for a jury trial that would be adjourned.

I liken the culture to *Game of Thrones*. Would I ever break free from a subculture that ran deep within Detroit's criminal justice system, from the judges to police, preachers, and politicians?

There's a "code of silence," but it's not what you think. While police officers are accused of keeping a culture that practices a code of silence—an understood rule in which one must withhold information to protect someone or something—this code, however, would be put to the test one day.

While picking up my check from the Eleventh Precinct, Officer Welton, a female officer I worked with, pulled me to the side. "I have something to tell you," she whispered. "Meet me in the locker room after you get your check."

"Okay," I said. Another letter. That was the first thing that crossed my mind. The shit was getting old.

I picked up my check and met Officer Welton in the locker room. "You said you wanted to see me? What's up?" I said, tucking my check in my purse.

"Sergeant Swatowski got a call from the West Bloomfield Police about you blackmailing a doctor for sex," she said.

I nearly fainted. "Blackmail? A doctor? Who?" I said, mentally trying to connect the dots.

"I don't know any details other than what I just told you. But please don't say anything because I overheard the phone conversation. I just wanted to give you a heads up."

Horrified, I asked, "When did this happen?"

"I think it was back in December, when you were assigned out for training."

"Okay. Thank you. I appreciate you looking out for me by telling me."

She nodded. She looked almost sorry for me.

"Thanks again," I said as I walked over to the exit.

Breaking her confidence, I immediately called the West Bloomfield Township Police Department and spoke with a man by the name of Detective Metcalf. He confirmed that one of his officers did in fact receive a phone call about me blackmailing a doctor for sex.

"When did this happen?"

He paused. I could hear him flipping through papers on the other end. Finally, he said, "December fourteenth, and I closed the case on December eighteenth."

"Is it possible you can fax that report over to me?" I asked.

"Absolutely. What's the fax number?"

I gave him my private fax number.

"Good luck," he said.

"Thanks," I said. I ended the call and headed straight for the front desk.

"Can I see the logbook?" I needed to view it to verify the details of the call. After all, everything that went down in the precinct was supposed to be recorded. It finally dawned on me that if we were ever going to get to the bottom of the harassment, I was going to be the one to lead the charge. After all, I was the one who had the most to lose.

I flipped through the logbook, using my right index finger to scan each entry. Nothing. I couldn't find anything related to the call. Another coverup, I guessed.

My mind raced as I drove home from the precinct. But if there was ever a day that things went from bad to worse, this was the day. Nicole called me on my cell phone.

"I'm on my way home, honey," I answered, skipping the usual "Yes, honey" greeting.

"Mom ..."

"Is everything all right?!" I could hear soft sobs on the other end of the phone.

"Some guy just called the house. And ... and—"

"And what? What did he say," I asked as I picked up speed.

"He said, 'Your mom sucks dicks and is the biggest hoe on the police department,'" she said, sobbing.

My truck swerved out of its lane. I grasped the wheel with both hands and steered my truck back into the lane. That was the straw that broke the camel's back. When you involve my daughters, all bets are off. I swallowed hard, fighting back tears, not of sorrow or sadness but of anger. "If he calls again, get the number off the caller ID."

"Okay," Nicole said. I could hear Marie and Yvette sobbing in the background too.

All I wanted to do in that moment was get to them and wrap my arms around them. Before I got my thoughts together regarding my next move, my mother called. She had received a call as well. You can imagine how embarrassed I was by this time. This was a large-scale attack coming from all angles and sides.

I had no choice but to tell my mother that I was being stalked by some crazed lunatic. I tried to make slight of it, but she wasn't buying it.

"Antionette, you have a dangerous job. I know you love it, but is it worth it?"

"Mom, I've dreamed about being a police officer ever since I was a little girl. Of course, everything has been worth it."

"Are you sure about that?"

"Yes, Mom," I tried to reassure her.

"'Cause the last time I checked, you had to let your daughters live with their dad and their jealous stepmother. Those girls have been practically raising themselves since they've been back at home. Maybe it's time you start weighing the pros against the cons."

"Mama, just support me right now. I'll do that. But if I quit now, that person wins. I cannot let whoever it is force me out. If and when I leave the force, it'll be on my terms, and my terms only."

"All right. I know I raised a strong-willed woman. But I just hope you don't let that strong will rob you and your girls out of the happiness you all deserve."

"I hear you, Mom. I hear you, but I have to go now," I said, trying to fight back tears.

There is nothing like a mother who can break it down to you just the way you need it. And that's what my mother did for me that day.

* * *

The following Monday, the shit hit the fan … again. I was summoned to the precinct by Officer Regis. I got there as quickly as I could. Officer Regis had made it into the station before me.

"Bostic!" she said, twirling her arms in the air.

"Yes?" I clenched my teeth and then released the hold … clenched them again and released the hold. "What is it now?" I said, letting her know I had some inkling of why I was summoned to the precinct.

"I got a picture of a naked woman's buttocks with a letter

attached with nasty comments about you in the mail. I made a copy and Sarg told me to put the original in evidence. Why would someone send me a letter?" she asked loudly, alerting a swarm of officers of her apparent contention.

"A picture. Of me? You have a naked picture of me?" I said, challenging the possibility.

"According to the sender, yes."

"Let's stop the games. I want to see the letter and the picture," I demanded.

By now, Officer Regis and the swarm of officers that had gathered around had all pissed me off.

Officer Regis held out the letter, and I snatched it out of her hand. I opened the envelope and retrieved the letter. This one was more humiliating than the others. The picture was explicit—a black nude female lying on her stomach with her buttocks and vagina exposed.

"This ... this is supposed to be me?" I said, holding the picture up. I swallowed hard. "This is not me ... you hear me?! It's not me! Somebody is after me!" I yelled, throwing the letter on the floor before storming off.

I could hear the faint sounds of the officers' chatter, chuckles, and gossip. I chose to keep walking. Then I had a sudden epiphany. I recalled leaving 36th District Court with Officer Regis, running into *him*, and introducing the two. The doctor that I was being accused of blackmailing for sex was the same doctor whose name was on the subscriber label on the magazine with the article titled "The Dark Art of Interrogation."

I turned back around. "I know who it is! I know who it is!" I screamed as I raced down the hallway back toward Officer Regis.

"Who? You know what?"

"I know who's been writing the letters, who sent the picture and cassette tape, and has been calling my family. He works in Narcotics! It's Officer Tracy. It's him."

"Do you have proof?" Officer Regis asked, scratching her head.

"I know it's him. I cut him off, and right after that, the letters started coming to the station."

"Now, you just have to prove it," Officer Regis said, her way of reminding me that I still had an uphill battle with proving my innocence and his guilt.

I was more determined than ever to fight and prove my innocence. I was not going to let Officer Tracy get away with destroying my character nor my dream. It was war, and I was ready to fight for my rights.

CHAPTER

19

CLUELESS

Where does a cop go for help when the people who are meant to keep you safe are the real danger? I couldn't share my pain because I was a cop, and cops were not supposed to whine, cry, or complain. Because I wore that blue uniform and carried a Glock, I was expected to be strong, cold, and almost non-caring. But that wasn't me at all, and I had fooled myself for buying into the silly notion.

The following day, I drove to the Detroit Police Department's Equal Employment Opportunity division. I was assigned to a woman by the name of Sergeant House, the investigator who would take my complaint. She escorted me down the narrow hall, into a room.

"Have a seat," she said, pointing to a chair in the small room. "I need you to fill out this harassment report. Make sure you include significant dates and details and identify involved persons, including any witnesses. Then, I'll record your interview when I return," she said before walking out and closing the door behind her.

It took me all of twenty minutes to complete the report, but it felt like hours had passed.

The door opened and the EEO investigator stuck her head in the room. "Done?"

"Yes, I am," I said, holding the report up.

She entered the room and closed the door again. Holding out her hand, she said, "I'll take that." Awkward silence filled the small room as she read the report. The crinkles in her forehead, the bewildered look on her face, and the wayward side of her lips complemented her unfriendly demeanor. I was annoyed by her pompous attitude.

When she finished, she looked up. "Did you ever tell him to stop sending you letters?" And before I could answer, she asked a follow-up question. "Did you report the incidents to your supervisors?"

"How can I report something if my supervisors are keeping silent about letters and calls from other police departments about me blackmailing a doctor for sex?" I said as humbly as I could in my own defense. "What the hell was I supposed to do? I obviously had no idea about what was going on behind my back. How could I?" I insisted. I was clueless.

"Look, there's a protocol in place. When it comes to harassment, you have to first tell them to stop before you have a case."

"How can I tell them to stop if I don't know who it is?"

"Sorry, that's the procedure."

I knew I wasn't going to get anywhere going back and forth with her. She was the cop I described, cold, almost non-caring. Her and her "You just fucked the wrong cop" attitude.

"Bostic. I want to ask you some background questions. That's okay with you?" she said, fiddling with the small recorder she'd laid on the table as she sat down in the chair across from me.

"Sure."

"How long did you and Officer Tracy date?"

"About two or three months."

"How would you describe your relationship?"

"It was cool. We went out a couple of times … had sex when I could. Our work schedules were different. I worked crazy hours and so did he."

"Were there problems?"

"Yes. He wanted to be in a serious relationship, mailing love letters about me being the only one for him, talking about marriage, and then he started accusing me of sleeping around and playing games. I wasn't thinking about anything long term."

"Did you know he was married?"

"Married? He told me he was divorced with two sons."

"Did you ever go to his house?"

"Go to his house for what? I worked crazy hours and sometimes didn't get off until three in the morning and just wanted a quick fix. So why would I go to his house?"

"Really? You didn't care about seeing where he lived?"

"We only dated for a few months. It wasn't that serious to me."

As the interview proceeded, the questions became more personal, almost embarrassing to have to answer. But I pushed through it, humiliation and all. As per protocol, she gave me some last-minute reminders. "Oh, by the way, don't contact any outside entities until I'm done with my investigation and Internal Affairs is done with theirs."

"How long will that be?" I asked as I stood.

"It could take months."

"Months?"

"Yes, months. We're backlogged. Join the party; you're one among many," she said with a smirk.

I left the interview outraged. I decided to call Ron Scott. I needed to find someone who'd believe my story ... believe me ... someone who was willing to break the code of silence, so to speak, in honor of truth.

Several weeks later, I received a call from Investigator Jamieson at the Domestic Violence Unit. He wanted me to meet him at a location away from his office.

"Why can't we meet at your office?" I said, suspicious that I might be getting set up.

"The department phone lines are tapped, recording all conversations."

His reason was good enough for me. I agreed to meet him, and we met at the corner of Cass and Forest.

"How have you been?" he asked when I walked up.

"Hanging in there, I guess."

"Good. That's good to hear." He looked around, scanning the area before continuing. "The reason I wanted to meet you is because I wanted to give you a heads up."

"Okay?" I said, anticipating bad news.

"The handwriting on the letters doesn't match the handwriting samples."

My jaw dropped. "I'm so sorry, Bostic." He paused again. "One more thing ... the Michigan State Police Crime Lab compared the writing on the envelopes, the writing in the letters, and those you provided from Officer Tracy ... they don't match either."

"I believe they do," I said, trying to remain calm. There was no way I was going to believe anyone else besides Officer Tracy was responsible for the letters, the cassette, and the picture. I was no fool by any stretch of the imagination. Since I had copies made, I had my own independent analysis by an expert handwriting specialist who got it done. And according to her findings, there was a perfect match. I shared the findings of my independent analysis with Investigator Jamieson.

"That might be the case, but it is going to be difficult to obtain any substantial evidence to file any charges for stalking or harassment."

"Why?" I challenged.

"They aren't allowing me to use your expert testimony to verify the anonymous writer as a witness. You don't have any solid evidence that will hold up in court that will prove that this officer, or whoever the person is, is truly out to get you."

As with Sergeant House, there was no sense in me going back and forth with Investigator Jamieson. I just had to be prepared to fight, and not just fight Officer Tracy but the corrupt system itself.

★ ★ ★

I cried in the shower most days. I was in severe emotional distress, and I didn't want the girls to see me in that state. Instead of seeking professional help, I self-medicated. The last thing I wanted to happen to me was for my psychological state of mind to be used against me. So I drank every night. I went to the strip clubs, picking up both men and women. It had been some time since I saw Strawberry, so I decided to inquire about her whereabouts.

"She doesn't work here anymore," a dancer named Candy said.

"Do you know where she's working?" I said, assuming she'd changed establishments.

"Nope. Like she vanished overnight," Candy said as she applied lip gloss on her lips.

Candy was pretty too, but she wasn't Strawberry; she wasn't as shapely, and she didn't have any exotic features either.

"Okay. Thank you," I said as I headed off and made my way back over to my table.

I ended up drinking myself into a stupor, taking a taxi back home, which was the same way I got to the strip club.

After letting myself in, I plopped down on the sofa in the front room. The moonlight shined through the sheer curtains, giving me just enough light to navigate over to the bar. I poured myself a glass of gin and tonic, something strong that would knock me right out.

How did I end up here? I thought as I walked over to the balcony. I wasn't new to the game. I mean, some of my partners that I had escapades with sat on the benches of justice, defended major court cases, played professional sports, owned reputable companies that had big connections with city officials, and wore brass as charms like a trophy or gold medal. No matter who it was, the understanding was always mutual—limited conversation, a little intimacy, and a thrilling battle to see who could climax first or last the longest. But little did I know it was too sophisticated of a game for me. I was just an amateur, and if I didn't know before, I came to know it now. I was in over my head.

I opened the sliding glass doors that led to the outdoor balcony. I could see the downtown area, lit with bright lights. I watched the ships on the river pass. I looked down … fourteen flights were a long way down. *Dare I go for it? And who would care? At least it'll be over. No more pain. No more embarrassment. No more having to defend myself. Jump!* But I didn't have the courage for that. *Maybe I could do something a little more daring, like take the precinct hostage … hold the key players at gun point. Tie and bind them to chairs, demanding that my story be put on the news so everyone in the city and world could see what had been done to me.* Yeah, that seemed like a good idea. I could force confessions out of them. I imagined myself sticking the barrel in their mouths so they could taste my pain and feel my desperation. "Confess! Confess! Confess!" That would be my demand. Get them all and for everything they'd done—violating the civil rights of the citizens, setting young black males up who were just driving while black, planting narcotics and weapons on the innocent … all just to get an arrest that would garner recognition from those in superior positions of power.

I imagined myself at the district court, walking the halls, searching for the man who was the mind and villain behind all the turmoil in my life. When I found him, I would grab him like a lion on its prey, pouncing and wrestling him to the ground, after handcuffing him and forcing him to come clean, admitting his culpability to writing the letters, harassing, stalking, and defaming me.

In all honesty, all of these would require meticulous planning and energy to carry out, which was time and energy I didn't possess. I thought maybe I could just take an easier way out, write a note to my family and other loved ones expressing and apologizing for my actions and taking my own life but explaining my pain and the thoughts that haunted me day and night. Then take my Glock, put it my mouth, pull and release the trigger. I would die instantly, never feeling a thing.

But then I imagined seeing my daughters weeping after having found my body, blood, and brains everywhere. How tragic and horrific. No, no, I couldn't do it … any of it. I couldn't leave my daughters in this type of pain and turmoil for the rest of their lives. It was time for me to admit my own part in the saga … my part in why I was now diving into a deep black hole.

The code of silence could be twisted to protect reputations of the favorited personnel, those who had been battle tested and tried. Those who had more to lose than I did.

As tears flowed, I walked back into the living room area, grabbed my cell phone from my purse and called one of my greatest advocates—my mother.

"Ma …" I sobbed.

"Ann?"

"Yes, it's me. No questions … just pray. Pray for me."

The call disconnected, and I knew what that meant. She was going to do just what I'd asked her to do—pray for me.

CHAPTER

20

I'M NOT IN DENIAL

I was assigned back to the Eleventh Precinct. My duties changed—no more playing dress up or protecting the mayor's wife and three sons. Nearly three years had passed, and I was still on the waiting list for the Evidence Tech Unit. There was no word from the investigators, the EEOC, nor the Domestic Violence Unit. Everything was still in limbo. I'd been told to put on my big girl panties and get over it because it happens to all of us—us being women, mostly.

What they could do, I couldn't do better. While members of the mayor's Executive Protection Unit were padding time sheets, drinking while on duty, and covering up accidents involving department vehicles without issue, I was not afforded the same shielded protection. I wasn't liked, and it wasn't just by Officer Tracy. Someone higher, with more power, didn't like me either. The rules didn't apply to me. Although I wore the badge and uniform, I had become an outsider, the black sheep of the "family."

I was reminded of a song they sang in church when I was growing up. The lyrics in the song include the words "There's trouble on every hand." And just like the lyrics in that song, in my world, there was trouble on every hand. It couldn't get any worse when Sergeant Kibble told me I was wanted for questioning by Internal Affairs.

"Bostic, I.A. wants you downtown. Take the scout car," he bellowed.

Maybe they have some updates on my sexual harassment case against Officer Tracy, I thought on the drive downtown.

I was greeted by a man by the name of Investigator Hunt who escorted me down a narrow hallway and into a small, cramped room, similar to the room I was in when I met with Sergeant House over at the EEO office. *Déjà vu.*

Tall and lanky, Investigator Hunt dropped the folder down on the table and folded his arms. "You might wanna have a seat," he said.

"Am I under arrest?"

"No, you're not under arrest, but if you leave, you will be. So I suggest you take a seat and just answer a few questions. It won't take long."

"Well, what is this about?" I asked, glancing over at the folder.

"I just want to ask you a couple of questions," he said, unfolding his arms and taking a seat on the opposite side of the table. "Have a seat," he said, pointing to the chair closest to me. "I'm going to read you your rights."

"My rights?"

"Yes, your rights."

This is serious, I thought. I pulled the chair out and sat down as Investigator Hunt turned on the recorder and read me my rights.

"Ready?" he said, raising his eyebrows.

I nodded.

"Do you own a green Ford Taurus?"

"No," I said, wondering where his line of questioning was going.

"Have you ever reported a car stolen?"

"No."

"Have you ever owned a green Ford Taurus?"

"No."

"Have you ever owned a Ford Taurus?"

"Yes."

"What color?"

"Black."

"Do you still have possession of that black Taurus?"

"No."

"What happened to the black Taurus?"

"I had a car accident."

"I need you to take me *through* the events of the accident. What I want to see is whether what you tell me adds up to what we have on record here," he said, opening up the folder

"To what you have?" I said, oblivious to what he was referring to.

"Yes. We got a call about you reporting a car stolen, filing a claim, and getting paid for it."

"I never reported a car stolen and got paid for it. I had a car accident, hit a fire hydrant, and my car was totaled out!" I emphatically stated.

"Whoa ... try to remain calm," he cautioned.

I swallowed hard.

"Is there any other information that you think would be helpful for our investigation?"

"No, I don't think so. It's pretty open and shut ... I had an accident."

He flipped through a few pages in the folder before asking the next question. "One more thing … other than what you've already identified, are you aware of any documents that might exist that corroborate what we've discussed so far?"

"There should be an accident report at the Ninth Precinct."

"Other than what we've already discussed, have you had any other problems or issues with your fellow officers or supervisors?"

I was bound to tell the truth. I had to say yes. "Yes," I said, biting my bottom lip. "I have a complaint of sexual harassment with the EEO. Sergeant House is the lead investigator for it. And I have a complaint with Domestic Violence, and Investigator Jamieson is over that one."

"Against who?"

"Officer Tracy in Narcotics."

I watched silently as he jotted down notes in response to my answers. And in robotic fashion, he asked another follow-up question. "Other than what we've already discussed, do you feel that the department has treated you unfairly in any other respect?"

Yes, was my answer, but without any representation, I thought it was best that I didn't answer the question, at least not truthfully. I didn't want to set myself up. After all, I was a cop not an attorney.

"I'd rather not answer that."

"Why?" he asked, peering over the rim of his eyeglasses.

"I don't have any representation. You did read me my rights, didn't you?" I wasn't that naïve that I was going to just walk right into any trap they laid for me.

"So, no answer?" he said, trying to clarify my position.

"No answer," I confirmed.

"Well, this pretty much wraps up my preliminary investigation. Do you have any questions?"

"Nope," I said, preparing to stand.

"I'll lead you out," he said, closing the folder as he stood from his seat.

*   *   *

"Stop that fucking crying!" he yelled. "It's all your fault, Bostic, because you forgot the rules, didn't you?" he roared as his hot breath steamed my face.

"Sir, yes, sir," I cried.

"Rule number two is 'Don't eat where you shit.' That's what I told you, didn't I?"

I didn't answer.

"But no, you go lose your damn mind on the job. Fucking around like you were the man with the dick. You're a woman in a man's world, the good ole boys club," he seethed with disgust. "Do you see where it got you? Nowhere! Now look at you!"

He was right. Everything he said was nothing but truth, truth that I could not deny. I stood paralyzed as he ranted on. "Bostic, you panicked in a situation. The car accident wasn't even your fault. I get that your salary wasn't shit and you couldn't afford the insurance; it's high as fuck in this city. But you let some slick, corrupt cop take you down the wrong side of the tracks. Now your dream job is on the line. And how could you forget rule number one? 'It's not what they call you; it's what you answer to.' You let that psycho cop, commander, sergeants, other officers, the mayor, and the chief get to you. It's unfortunate that you got caught up in the crime, corruption, and coverups at DPD. I hope you survive this," he said, his eyes piercing. Everything Carter said was right.

Survive. Survive. Survive. I heard the words faintly as I struggled to move. My legs felt like lead, but I tried with all my strength.

"Fight, Antoinette. Fight," I repeated until, finally, I woke up. My gown was drenched. A dream. It was just a dream. I was in my bedroom. I could hear the faint sounds of the television in the living room where the girls were. My girls. I crawled out of bed and opened my bedroom door. I had to lay my eyes on my girls. They were all I had. If I didn't want to live for myself, I owed it to Nicole, Marie, and Yvette to live for them.

Softly, I closed my bedroom door and leaned my weak body against it. *You've got to fight this thing, Antoinette.* "I know," I whispered. "I know. I will," I promised myself.

CHAPTER

21

BOARDWALK

"I'll buy that for four hundred dollars," I said, waving my money at the banker. I loved the game Monopoly as a kid, especially when I purchased the most sought-after property on the Monopoly board: Boardwalk, the property that's located between GO and Luxury Tax spaces, and when paired with Park Place, would complete the dark blue property set. Buying Boardwalk was essentially high-risk and a high reward. It was also the most dangerous square to land on if owned by someone else. The rent that was required was expensive and could instantly bankrupt you.

Although I never knew what "chance" card life would deal me, it was more than money challenges and property obstacles that I would have to navigate to win the game. It seemed like my life was much like Monopoly, as my world turned into a mesmerizing world of ups and downs, wild events, unforeseen challenges, and still, a chance to win and win big.

The urban metropolis was a cesspool of corruption. I had every reason to believe that the chief, the clergy, and the mayor were all after me in retaliation for the sexual harassment claim against that scumbag Officer Tracy and the arrest of one of their own, a pastor, in a prostitution sting. Not to forget to mention the report regarding the chaos at the mayor's mansion. The code of silence was to be enacted to protect them all. Now, treated as an outcast, I had to fend for myself. My job, my reputation, and my sanity were all on the line.

★   ★   ★

The morning I had to go before the trial board, I woke up with a throbbing headache. I lay in bed even after my alarm had gone off. My hands were trembling, my feet tingled, and everything sounded muffled as if I were underwater. I couldn't concentrate. I wished it was all just a long dream, a nightmare I would wake up from, because this wasn't just about me. It was also about my livelihood, which would ultimately affect my girls. And I couldn't let them down. I vowed to fight, and there was no going back.

I got up, took a refreshing shower, dressed, and mentally prepared myself to tackle the day. Before paisley blue skies would be kissed by the pink sunrise, I could hear the lyrics to Fred Hammond's song, "No Weapon," play in my head—*No weapon formed against me shall prosper ... It won't work.* And it gave me the power I needed to push through the day.

Once in my car, I took a deep breath, placed my foot on the brake, turned the key in the ignition, and backed out of my parking space.

Following the marble floors in the Internal Affairs building felt nothing like following the Yellow Brick Road. I was definitely no longer in Ypsilanti. The room where the hearing took place was more like a board room, with an oval table that seated twelve police department brass and their attorneys, who would present their case, evidence, and even recommend disciplinary action for conduct unbecoming of an officer. The oval table also accommodated my appointed union attorney who would defend me, my actions.

Likened to a rigorous tennis match between Venus and Serena Williams, the back-and-forth accusations versus defense was on full display, and there was no judge to use his gavel and take control.

"Anyone knows that car insurance in the city of Detroit is highway robbery!" My attorney thundered as he pounded the table. And on a rookie's twenty-five-thousand-a-year salary for protecting and serving the streets, my client had to choose between rent, paying her car note, expenses, and feeding her daughters!"

"Let's remember that Officer Bostic lied and covered up an accident," the City of Detroit's attorney countered.

"Let's not forget that officers in this department have done worse and are still on the job today!" my union attorney rebutted. He was sharp. I just hoped he was skilled enough to beat the crooked system.

"Let's remember that Officer Bostic lied twice in Garrity."

"Let's not forget that maybe she was trained to plead the Fifth, especially when sent without union representation," my attorney defended.

Then the worst thing I could have imagined was introduced—details of my sexual escapades over the years. Yes, I learned on this day that there was no such thing as "kiss but don't tell." They all told, explicit details and all. The only thing I could do was sit there. Yet, I could still hear that small voice saying, *"No weapon formed against thee shall prosper."*

When the trial board was over, I hurriedly left the room and made a mad dash for the elevators. Attempting to drown out any noise, I placed my index fingers in my ears. When the elevator doors opened in the parking deck, I darted out and raced to my car. The drama and pressure were more than I had anticipated. I couldn't wrap my head around being set up by my family in blue. I was scared. I wanted my mom.

I managed to unlock my car door, and once inside, I leaned my head against the steering wheel and began to weep. Waves of sorrow seemed to engulf me, seemingly suffocating the life out of me. I was on a roller coaster of guilt, despair, hopelessness, loss, loneliness, helplessness, isolation, and fear, and I couldn't seem to catch my breath. The agonizing, emotional pain was so deep. My hands shook; my vision was blurred by the flood of tears; my black eyeliner and mascara trickled down my face. I knew I looked like Bozo the Clown, in more ways than one. I felt as though they were all laughing at me. In that moment, I knew how the character Carrie felt on her prom night in the movie *Carrie*. *"They're all gonna laugh at you,"* played in my head. And if I possessed the power that she had, I would have eviscerated the entire Internal Affairs building that day.

After taking a quick look in the car mirror, I leaned my head back against the headrest and allowed life to take me back in time. My mind began to travel through a time warp, to where it all started when I was a kid. My memories had been long ago colored by the blues and other misfortunes, and I just couldn't seem to get a break. I also reminisced on all the good times within the last ten years. And as if I was literally driving, I could see each street and the memories that were made on them. From Woodward Ave to Madison and passing 36th District Court, which was home to the Judge's chambers and his Handgun Intervention Protection Program, a program dedicated to saving the lives of young men in the city from gun violence. I was proud to be part of an amazing grass roots mission.

Then, through Greektown, where I'd take long walks during the summer to enjoy ice cream with the girls or a girls' night out with Bernadette at Flood's. Then onto East Jefferson, passing the Click, the best hole-in-the-wall breakfast spot, where some of everyone ate. I loved their stemmed potatoes and crispy bacon. And of course, there was Chene Park—the best place on earth for live concerts, from jazz to R&B. I'd ride down Winder Street and stroll past the Manoogian Mansion, *The place where so many lies and cover ups occurred*, I thought.

Onward to Belle Isle. The city's gem was like a maze, sitting on the banks of the Detroit River, the vacation spot for the Grand Prix. Oh, and I couldn't forget the Giant Slide. Working Vice, we'd catch people having sex in their cars on the hood. I recalled rolling up on a man with his pants down, having sex with a transgender person, and when he turned around, he was wearing a clergy collar; the things people do in the dark.

Heading west on Jefferson toward Hart Plaza, I smiled, remembering being assigned out to Summer Jams for Nicole's eighteenth birthday celebration. She had a blast with her cousins, and I was able to get backstage so they could see the entertainers. It was the icing on the cake for Nicole.

Making a slight right, I passed Wayne County Community College on Fort Street. I wondered how many young women were seduced by the professors while innocently pursuing their dreams … like me. I was sure I wasn't the only one.

Southwest Detroit; the Third Precinct was like family. Michigan Ave was the runway of strip clubs and Tailways. Onto I-94 East, to the Lodge exit, Wayne State University, past 4500 University Towers, our old apartment during my college days, then Eastern Market. I loved the fresh fruits and vegetables, flowers and food. The atmosphere was always festive.

Oh, there was my old apartment located at 3641 Russell, and blocks away was the Wayne County Medical Examiner's Office, the location where I went to hell and came back. I zoomed past the DIA then to the New Center Area, Fitness Works, and Career Works, places I could call home, places where I discovered that we were all beautifully flawed, working on our imperfections together while serving and assisting others along the way. Finally, onto the Eleventh Precinct, where I would be re-introduced to the rules of the game.

Detroit, the city of light and darkness, where all my dreams came true and the nightmares too. I learned so much about life and death and that money can't buy you happiness. Nevertheless, I was satisfied in knowing that it could buy my girls ice cream on a hot summer day. I wasn't perfect, but whatever I did, I gave it my best.

I knew this was not supposed to be how my dream career ended. The code of silence, the isolation, and the deception were all caving in on me. In that very moment, I knew in my spirit that my journey as a Detroit police officer was coming to an end.

I pondered the questions once again. *Why else would they wait two years later? Who could be after me?* I would not know the answers to either one of these questions. Slowly, I lifted my head from the headrest, dried my eyes, started my ignition, and put the gear in drive.

I headed down Interstate 94 East to Downtown Detroit and found myself in front of the Wayne County Community College administration building located on Fort Street. I needed to speak with my only sister, Bernadette. I reached for my cell and called her.

"Hey, Bern. Can you come outside?"

"What's the matter?" Bernadette said, sensing my somber tone.

"Just come outside!" I screamed.

Before I knew it, Bernadette came running outside and hopped in my truck. "What's the matter?" she asked again.

The sea of tears commenced again. "Nobody sees me."

"I see you," Bernadette consoled.

"Do you?" I said.

"Yes, I do," Bernadette said, reaching her arms out to embrace me.

And that's when I spotted him. "That's him, Bern!"

"That's who?" she said, looking around.

It was him. I couldn't even begin to describe the shock and hysteria at seeing Officer Tracy driving his O.J. Simpson Black Bronco, heading toward us—Westbound on Fort. His piercing eyes darted as he passed. Then he made an abrupt U-turn.

"Did you see that, Bern?! He's after me!" I screamed, pulling my gun out of its holster.

"What are you doing?!" Bernadette screamed. She was scared too.

"I'm going to get him before he gets us!" I said as I watched Officer Tracy drive past. This time, he was pointing at me with his trigger finger like a gun as if he were aiming to shoot me.

"The police, the mayor, and the preacher are all out to get me!" Wildly pointing my gun out the window, I felt my entire body trembling in fear. "Nobody is helping me ... nobody sees me!" I screamed.

CHAPTER

22

SEASONS

E very season has something unique that makes it special. Winter, spring, summer, and fall—I love them for their own uniqueness.

Winter's white snow coats the trees; glittering icicles sparkle as they hang off the branches like diamonds, and dancing flakes fashion a Winter Wonderland preparing for Christmas. In spring, the sky is clear, and winds are refreshing. There's a scent of new in the air; new leaves come out of trees, tulips and flowers bloom, and butterflies quietly flutter. Passover and Easter commemorate Jesus Christ's death, burial, and resurrection.

Summer, when Memorial Day kicks off, with hot fun and sun-kissed days, blue skies with cotton candy clouds, splashes in the pool and the laughter of children playing in the park. Grilled hot dogs and July 4th fireworks close out the holiday. Fall is the premier of God's artwork as green leaves are painted dazzling colors of rich ambers, jazzy reds, glimmering golds, dazzling yellows, and earthy browns, welcoming Halloween and Thanksgiving. While I loved them all, each season came with resentment; each season had its personalized natural disaster. Winter brought blizzards and below-freezing temperatures. Spring carried torrential rains and flooding, tornados, drought. Summer shared spring's tornados and flooding but owned the sweltering heat, tropical storms, and hurricanes. Fall shared all three. My professional, personal, and parenting life seemed to relate to each one.

After much negotiation, I found myself back at Chene Park, the one place where I'd made the choice to follow my dreams of becoming a Detroit cop. I parked and walked the sidewalk to stand at the water and look toward the Renaissance Building, the Ambassador Bridge, and the Lighthouse.

I stood at the river for hours, watching the cargo ships and sailboats pass, questioning how a city like Detroit could spawn one of the most infamous scandals in its history. Where Motown Records birthed greats like Marvin Gaye, the Jackson Five, the Queen of Soul Aretha Franklin, K.E.M., and the Clark Sisters. Music, for me, was not about Soul, R&B, or Gospel, but there were certain days when I needed the lyrics, other days the beat, and then at other times, I needed them both.

My career would be in the hands of the Detroit Police Board of Commissioners, who was in charge of the Detroit Police Department officers' mistakes regarding policy and rules, budget approval, officer discipline, and citizen complaints. I soon learned that out of the Board of Police Commissioners' eleven members, seven were elected from each police commission district and four were appointed by the mayor.

I might as well turn in my badge and gun, because those four appointed by the mayor outweigh the power of the seven, I thought to myself. But I wasn't going down like that. I returned to the Eleventh

Precinct on midnights; my daughters, sister, mother, and myself were living in fear, not knowing what would happen next. I moved my daughters from Downtown Detroit to downriver, where they would be safe. Months passed without any word from the department: Internal Affairs, EEOC, Domestic Violence, or Officer Tracy. *Is this the calm before the storm?*

Work didn't get easier; the officer continued to stalk me. Instead of letters, he drove by the Eleventh Precinct, pulling up along-side me anywhere at any time, and I still got no response or assistance. The prosecutor's office didn't help; Attorney Kym Worthy wouldn't respond to any of my emails. Even the Detroit Police Officer Association claimed they couldn't intercede on my behalf because of us being officers.

Out here, observations serve better than analysis. Cops are first responders, patrolling the streets to protect and serve people, dispatched to calls of violence in progress, the first ones on the scene and eyewitnesses to death. Cops are not surgeons, and crime prevention and police reform are as vital as criminal apprehension, which takes powerful eyes and deeper instincts. I realized I had both.

I wish it were that easy. The days, weeks, months, and years showed me how to patrol when I began to see the streets differently. Instead of questioning why things happened, I could see the reasons for the why. I didn't see people the same anymore. I didn't see abandoned houses as urban blight. What I could see was broken families of domestic violence and drug abuse and poverty due to lack of education and unemployment. Even the absent men in the homes were not by choice either but design. With the black man in mind, incarceration or death related to selling narcotics or gun violence. I didn't see a suspicious man loitering or a group of teens too young to be walking the streets when they should be in school. I saw a possible

Vietnam vet suffering from PTSD or a group of teens whose mom might be on drugs and father in prison.

Across the city, eyes were windows to the soul. I would see the prostitutes, women and men, black or white, ranging from the late teens to their fifties, exposing their breasts as short shorts showcased butt cheeks. Others were battered as if they had been in a fight with Mike Tyson. Many thin women in their twenties were living a dangerous life that required them to work from early evening to five o'clock in the morning, wandering through some of the most dangerous streets and corners that would lead them to just blocks from the border, separating the U.S. and Canada—the City of Detroit.

I could see their grief and trauma. I saw their rage and their anger, that's for sure. But I also saw their fear and distress. I watched all the ways they were acting out all the behaviors I'd seen in myself live and in living color. They were victims of their circumstances that stemmed from some form of abuse or trauma that occurred at some point in their lives. To cope, they were now attempting to numb the pain of their past. I knew all too well that "fixes" never fixed anything. You must put in the hard work. There are no shortcuts to emotional healing and wellness.

There were moments I took in between runs to speak with the women. What was once from the eyes of a child's dream come true would now be the sight of the pain I was living through. The blue code of silence changed me. Nothing just happens. I noticed that I walked differently; I talked to people differently. I had changed. I was coming from a place of compassion, not the arrogance that many cops have. I realized that I wasn't one of them. It wasn't about commanding power and control or wearing the badge and carrying a gun; it was about the people.

While I was armed and had to protect myself and my family from the drive-bys that occurred from dusk until dawn. I had to make sure my girls were safe. It was my only option because I had no help. I couldn't let my girls see me living in fear, even though I was crumbling inside. I felt overwhelmed and lost in the web that connected the three—police, preachers, and politicians. *Is it my cross to carry?* I wondered.

It seemed as if I couldn't escape life. *Has everything that is happening to me already been determined or predestined?"* I wondered. *Is it all part of a bigger picture?* I began to stand up for myself despite the gender-related comments and jokes that were made in my presence. I watched as other female officers participated in the jokes. And because gender-related jokes were part of the good ole boy's club culture within the police department, they went unreported due to fear of harassment and the associated risk of ruining future career opportunities, especially upward mobility.

Once I made my mind up to move beyond the victim mindset, there was no stopping me. I was not what happened to me. My identity had been stunted since I was a little girl. I was referred to as "Marlene Junior," after my mother. I was told I'd never be anything, just like both of my parents, that there was no escaping my DNA. But again, I had to put the focus back on my daughters and return to being a cop. I felt as though I was able to be myself ... no cops and robbers or handcuffs, just me. I was now playing by the rules, but the rules weren't working in my favor.

"Looks like my life is over at the ripe age of thirty-five," I said to my twin sister, Bernadette. It was the end of another season.

★　★　★

Usually, at this time of the year, I'd be tanned from hanging out at the water park with the girls. Instead, however, I was lying in bed depressed. Bernadette sat across from me on the window ledge. I was lucky too, because in addition to being my twin, she was also one of my closet friends. We had both weathered quite a few storms together. Her life hadn't exactly followed the perfect route either. Our lives were ironically parallel, except I had the lead on her in experience by ten years.

"How do you know your life is over? How do you know this is the end? Can you foretell the future?" Bernadette said as she eyed me calmly from the window ledge.

"What?" I asked defensively. "I dreamed of being a cop or mortician since I was a kid. Yeah, I worked at the morgue as an autopsy technician. Check. And as a cop, I worked Vice Unit undercover, Executive Protection Unit for the mayor, certified Crime Scene Investigation ..." I hesitated for a moment and then blurted it out. "It's obvious; the police, preacher, mayor, and the stalker are after me."

Bernadette paused, measuring her words, and then said, "I wonder what would happen if you quit trying to be ordinary and just be you ... just where you are and stop chasing life and live? We are mirror twins, unique in more ways than one. You might be surprised." She laughed. "Maybe life as you know it has shifted. But just because you're feeling defeated doesn't mean you've lost."

She was right; it wasn't the end. When my phone rang, it was my mother on the other end.

CHAPTER

23

THE LIGHT OF DAY

"Code blue; we've lost her."

Code Blue? We've lost who?

If you can't wake up from a nightmare, maybe you're not asleep! Have you ever had a dream that felt so real? It's not that you wake up one day with a chill in your soul and a troublesome sense of perplexity. You know where you are; you just don't know who you are. I wondered who that person in the mirror was as I stared back, looking at her then looking *in* her. *What have I done and how did I get here?*

In the distance, on that early spring morning, I had a vision. I could vividly see Bernadette looking at her watch. My girls were standing in separate corners of the room as they all waited in silence. Growing anxiety filled the waiting room for any words of an update. When the man in the white coat hesitated and the lines on his face deepened, Bernadette stood, paralyzed from head to toe. The color in her face disappeared.

I could see and hear. "Am I ...?" I asked. The words felt like a dagger piercing my chest cavity. The attempted "I'm sorry," explanation stole Bernadette's breath from her lungs. My eyes followed as he towered over me.

As the bright lights flashed beyond my eyelids. I didn't want to open my eyes, but I suddenly remembered I was in the Detroit Receiving Hospital emergency room. I reached for the badge hanging from a chain in the pool of blood; it pressed red-hot against my hand. Each gasp tore down my throat and my mind raced as I lost myself in the storm. I saw me through the blur of motion and color. I followed the doctor. I walked closer to see and tell myself goodbye, but it wasn't me.

My nightmare was real. When I blinked the heaviness from my eyes, I would find the answers.

I woke up in a cold sweat, shaken. The sunrise graced the blue sky; the breeze from the window was like the wind off the ocean. On bended knees, I began to cry, struggling to pray. I was confused, no doubt. I knew that whatever it was that was also stalking me was bigger than me. It was bigger than asking God, "Is this real? Please help ... lead me. Guide me to what I'm supposed to write, in Jesus' name, amen."

In a quickened moment, I was back in my room, in my bed. It wasn't me lying cold on the table in the emergency room. It was her—Tammara Green—a beautiful young lady, mother, and daughter ... the woman also known as "Strawberry."

My mind immediately recalled the night dispatch called out the run. There was a disturbance at the Manoogian Mansion ... the mayor's mansion. The VIP guest list for the party at the mansion included police officers, prominent businessmen, and politicians, as well as renowned clergy. And Strawberry was there. What did she know? What did she see? Had she been killed to prevent exposing those on the VIP list? Was she the sacrificial lamb, killed to send a message to others to keep their mouths closed? Most likely.

No. She can't be gone. I dashed to the bathroom as the sun blossomed between the bathroom window blinds. Tears escaped my ducts in a Niagara Falls fashion. I looked in the mirror. The reflection from the light shining through the blinds mixed with the salt-filled tears glistened like diamonds.

I turned on the shower, hoping that in some magical way, it would wash away my tears and my pain. My world was crashing in on me, it seemed. I had a very powerful enemy in the world. I fell to the floor and began pounding on it. I tried to whisper a word of courage, but my strength seemingly left me on the bathroom floor. Even as I attempted to stand, my legs felt like jelly. My throat held back something between a sob and a scream.

My imagination made connections that appeared unreal at first, but I couldn't seem to let go of them. A kind of confidence ignited within me.

I began to question the visions of my dream. It was me, but it wasn't. Maybe the stress and fear of the unknown was a relentless underlying force in my life; All of it, from the stalker, to the sexual harassment, the trial board, and losing focus of my three daughters, was a sign of me fighting for survival, sexual problems, and the pain inflicted by the blue code of silence connected to me and overall corruption in Detroit. There were good days and depression days, when I wanted to run away from it all, or was this my moment of awakening to life Behind the Badge?"

"That wasn't just me in the Detroit Receiving trauma room; it wasn't just my story. I found myself in the kitchen preparing Starbucks mocha coffee and grabbing my laptop. I don't even remember how I got there; I must have been on autopilot. So many thoughts, memories, situations, and similarities were racing through my mind as to how her life came to an end.

I began scouring the internet for her story. I searched on sites like Defrosting Cold Cases, NewsOne, Dlive, Clickondetroit, Reddit, CBSDetroit, WXYZ.com, and csafd.proboards, a site dedicated to victims of violent crimes.

The next link called Deadline Detroit told of a flashy young mayor, a party at his mansion (maybe, maybe not), an exotic dancer named after a speckled fruit, his reportedly crazy wife, and a fatal drive-by four months later—all real-life factors.

A common thread in all the stories was the possible coverup of the murder of the exotic dancer, Tammara Green … Strawberry. And how an exotic dancer toppled Detroit's hip-hop mayor, describing her as a "dichotomy," two distinctly different people. Rumor was that she was blessed with a body that was a masterpiece by God. She was the definition of a striptease artist, seducing powerful men in politics, the corporate giants, criminal justice leaders, pastors, and drug lords running the streets.

God as my witness, by my second cup of coffee, I had dialed in. There was no light at the end of the tunnel; it was light everywhere. It's like I had known her my whole life. The more I read about her, the details of the story, all I could hear was the message in my nightmare, *Tell my story,* as a literal crime scene was unfolding in my sleep.

"I was there that night!" I cried. I was suddenly pulled back in time. I was a rookie working midnights at the Third Precinct when dispatch called for scout cars to make the Manoogian Mansion—the mayor's residence that was under renovation. My partner and I didn't make it, but so many officers did, along with other VIP guests.

I remembered her. I never forgot a pretty face. The night we answered the call to a disturbance at the strip club. I met her ... we had an encounter or two. I felt our lives connecting in so many ways; we were both victimized, manipulated, used, betrayed, and abandoned by those we trusted, introduced to a world that would shatter our youth, highly traumatized by the very people and system meant to protect us. We both had the same determination to be successful, attempting to improve our lives and rise above our situations, escape by any means necessary, not just for ourselves but our three children.

Our lives were parallel. I couldn't get it out of my head. Why was I privy to all of this, I wondered. She wasn't any of my business. It struck me as odd that I could relate to Tamara's story, a stranger, having walked a mile in her shoes, her shame, my shame, our experiences in the game. I saw our truth ... our ugly truth.

I was horrified by the unimageable trauma she experienced that visited me in my dreams. While she didn't survive, I did.

Rest in peace, Strawberry ...

★   ★   ★

I forced myself to read through all of Officer Tracy's letters mailed to the Detroit Police Department personnel and myself, the police reports, the expert handwriting analysis compared to that of the state police. I was going back in time, trying to wrap my mind all around this psycho thriller; my life was like a Hollywood movie.

A lot of what I did and how I reacted was a direct effect of the world I was groomed to live in, and I discovered that the answers to many questions were like pieces to a puzzle that stemmed from greed, pride, and silence, a code our country lives by.

I started to read through the pages of my journal. My eyes

skimmed over the written words of advice spoken to me by women in brass:

- Don't fuck down, only up. Be with someone who can help you and your career.
- Don't settle for less. Be in control. Be a lady at all times.
- Don't hang out at bars or clubs. Be careful who you're with.
- Don't listen to bullshit. Associate with positive people.
- Have a plan. Work on being promoted. Have your stuff together, wrapped real tight.
- You're not the only one; it happens to all of us.

Standing at the shores of the Detroit River, I marveled at the Detroit skyline and closed my eyes to hear autumn's crisp leaves rustle in the wind, taking a deep breath. "I have to make a decision," I whispered. I wanted to be successful so badly. I wanted to live, make my daughters, my mother, and siblings so proud of me, but instead, I had run back in the dark and headed for self-destruction. I would find sticky notes in the bathroom, on my windshield with the word "Snitch" written on them. I was fearful for my life.

On the cold morning of January 17, 2006, I found myself standing at the rocks at the outer banks of the Detroit River at Chene Park. There was always something about the water that drew and captivated me. It was a place where I made several life-changing decisions, including the decision to become a Detroit police officer.

I swear I'd been there before, except this time, it was winter, same place but different season and time. To the left, right, and forward, all I could see was a river covered in a large, dark sheet of ice, with the suns reflection of the sky locked in like a mirror, when something grabbed my attention. I could also see the Renaissance Center-GM

Headquarters, the Ambassador Bridge, and the Lighthouse; they were all looking back at me. I was awake, awakened to the corruption that I was exposed to, engaged, and now endangered. Would my demise be at the hands of forces bigger than me?

I was forced to look at the woman in the mirror, to lose everything, to fall on my face in front of my daughters, family, and the city I served—Detroit. The lessons I learned on my journey were tools I would need on the road of purpose to my destiny.

There was something so wrong and appalling about it all, all that goes on behind the badge. In the distance I heard the wailing of a police car. I began to cry. Something had died inside me. For me, hell was cold, like going into the freezer at the Wayne County Medical Examiner's Office to pull a body out from under ten other corpses; it was bone chilling. What was happening was a cleansing of the mind, body, and soul. Soon the giants that were after me would fall. I closed my eyes and waited for it to happen.

I stood at the river for hours, watching the cargo ships pass, shattering the ice, full speed ahead. I didn't know what to do or where to go; there was nowhere to hide. As a Detroit cop, I could see death all around me.

*　*　*

I hereby notify the Detroit Police Department that I resign from active service. I fully understand the department policy on reinstatement. I recognize that the submission of this notification is binding and that it may not be rescinded unless expressly approved by the chief of police.

I turned in my badge and police photo identification, handed over my department-issued 9mm Glock and magazines. I was given a pen to sign on the blue line, one of the hardest things I'd ever had to do. I resigned.

That knot in my throat was suffocating and I was fighting to breathe. I was angry and frustrated by the department's bullshit and the good ole boys network connected to the church and politicians; they were the criminals who showed me the way.

My childhood dreams of being a cop and saving the city had come to a sobering end. Interestingly enough, however, in my gut, I felt my purpose had been completed through my assignments ... Strawberry was one of them.

Not all superhero's wear capes. They are selfless in serving their community. Thank you, Cousin Ray for being on the front lines. I appreciate your dedication to service.

AFTERWORD

ehind the Badge: Her Story is Antoinette's entire soul path to enlightenment—her journey; what a page turner. It probably was not written with that intention.

The story starts with Detroit as the backdrop to Antoinette's quest with her three young daughters, living out a childhood dream that turned into a nightmare, spiraling downward, the cycles of destiny, the cycle of errors and lessons learned. It also represents her inquiry into spiritual beliefs of life and death, heaven, hell, and the soul. It is also interesting to note that *Behind the Badge: Her Story* begins as an outwardly expanding spiral where she finds herself evolving, the soul ascending from questions of reality into the spirit world, where she starts her journey seeking a higher truth.

During her journey with her young three daughters, Antoinette respectively searches for a reason, a heart, and courage needed to complete her quest for enlightenment. After surmounting many obstacles, she finally reaches Detroit, chasing her destiny. Antoinette certainly has a story to tell. Her experiences are remarkable, some dangerous and scary, some shocking and difficult, and some healing.

As you read her story, you'll probably came to identify with some of the experiences Antoinette shares because something similar has happened to you. You may have realized that you are not alone. Antoinette did not have this benefit. She was left to solve almost every problem on her own.

The problem could be discrimination against one's own group, rape, still-taboo lesbian relationships, harassment, teen pregnancy, childcare crises, corruption, betrayal, or prostitution.

"I was born as what they called an identical mirror twin ..."

"...but women seem to have the power to manipulate. A woman with a pretty face and curves can run the world. I have done some things that I pray every day God forgives me for ..." [Antoinette's dad]

"The man is just being nice and trying to show you a good time."

"You'll be nothing. You're just like your mama—she was nothing."

"Above all, we were taught to always keep God first."

"Growing up in church played a significant part in my life as a child."

"The life of double standards—the lies and betrayals coming from people in the church whom I trusted and respected..."

"'Daddy! Mama! Stop!' My legs crumbled, and we fell to the floor. I could see the girls standing on the stairs, crying. Nicole was holding Yvette and Marie was hanging on to her."

"Sex was used as a presentation to entertain those in power and control to get quickly promoted."

"My emotional turbulence when it came to relationships was reflected by the number of men I dated simultaneously. I had a date every day of the week and others to meet whatever needs I had."

"'I don't have any help watching the girls while I go to work, and I need you to take them into your house with your new family,' I said,

dropping off the three girls with just a few minutes' notice. 'Mommy will be back for you.'"

"It was difficult for me to fathom that police drive around in pursuit of a young black male target as a prize."

"So, if you ever happen to approach a scene at a strip club or bar and you see anyone blue or a prominent public official, look the other way."

"I had every reason to believe that the chief, the clergy, and the mayor were all after me in retaliation for the sexual harassment claim against Officer Tracy and the arrest of one of their own, a pastor, in a prostitution sting."

"I felt overwhelmed and lost in the web that connected the three—police, preachers, and politicians."

The brains, the heart, and the courage needed to complete Antoinette's quests were found within. Throughout the story, her "inner voice," her intuition, would be her guiding light on her quest to salvation.

This leads to her ultimate revelation and, with the help of God (her divine guide), she finally sees everything she ever wanted or could be found "in her own backyard."

To obtain enlightenment, Antoinette had to conquer from within her amendments, answers, failures, beliefs, confusions, misguided information, and denials from her childhood to adult life.

At the end of the story, Antoinette wakes up, magnificently combining her physical and spiritual lives. She has now seen the light, being herself again and realized that life is parallel, that nothing just happens, and she can finally say that *Behind the Badge: Her Story* is not just about me but *her.* "I lived to tell our story."

Antoinette's story, from page one until the end, will stay with you as you think about it over and over as it has with me. I am hoping it will help you with your story.

Elizabeth Landers, Author

The Script: The 100% Absolutely Predictable Things Men Do When They Cheat, (co-author)

The Affair Playbook: What Happens in an Affair? How Angelina Jolie & Brad Pitt's Divorce Provides Some Insights

Upcoming, Child Abuse: What to Do When
It Turns Out That the People We Trust Can No Longer Be Trusted

ABOUT THE AUTHOR

While many unfortunately feel lost and defeated in the fight for their voices to be heard, Antoinette James has made a commitment to fight for those who seemingly have no voice at all. Today, this former Detroit police officer has tirelessly served as an advocate for victims of crime in the Detroit

Metropolitan areas of Wayne, Oakland, and Macomb counties for the past three years.

Antoinette James holds a Bachelor of Applied Science in Criminal Justice where she made the dean's list during her tenure at Ferris State University. In 2016, she received the Ferris State University College of Education & Human Service Criminal Justice Annual Scholarship as well as honorable recognition at University of Michigan-Dearborn. She is a member of N.O.B.L.E (National Organization for Black Law Enforcement Executives) and serves as chaplain for the International Fire and Police Association.

Twelve years ago, Antoinette and her husband, Anthony James, felt compelled to answer a call that placed their one-month-old grandson, Prince Jerald, into their care as foster parents. They were unprepared to parent a baby again. In fact, their youngest daughter was graduating high school. They searched for foster and adoption resources and advocated for quality and affordable resources. They were able to adopt their grandson, and four years later, they adopted his younger brother also. Antoinette is thankful for the many agencies and mentoring programs that helped them along the way. "We wouldn't change our lives for the world. We feel that the smile on our grandsons' faces and hearing, 'I love you,' is what life's all about."

In 2012, Antoinette returned to Detroit as an Ameri Corps Vista volunteer to assist in building the Detroit Youth Violence Prevention Initiative (DYVPI), an organization that prevents youth violence in Detroit through positive youth development and engagement. In the same year, she was hired to work at the Children's Aid Society to provide case management at Cody and Osborn High Schools' Safety Stations, where she could help remove barriers to student safety. She was also hired to work at Detroit Ceasefire, a program that was first implemented in Boston in 1996 and documented in the book *Don't Shoot* by David M. Kennedy. Between May 1996 and the end of 1998, the Ceasefire program has been found to show a nearly sixty-three percent reduction in homicide victimization among those aged twenty-four and under and a fifty percent reduction in homicide among all age groups in Boston. The program has been referred to as the Boston miracle. And if anyone knew Detroit needed a miracle, Antoinette did.

Antoinette James has made it her mission to ensure that people who are socially vulnerable have a voice and justice is served on their behalf. Antoinette isn't just an agent of change in her community and city—she's leaving an impact on the world that cannot be easily erased. Through both her professional and personal experiences, Antoinette has been afforded the opportunity to experience life on both sides of the fence. Complete with her educational background, life challenges, and experience on the force, she's transformed into a *force* to be reckoned with.

RESOURCES

What to do if you're a victim of a crime or if you're the survivor of an attempted homicide:

We suggest you choose the hotline that is best for you. If you aren't sure which helpline, in Southeast Michigan contact Open Arms (313-369-5780) to speak with a crime victim advocate or therapist. They can talk to you about which helpline might fit your needs and discuss additional options and/or resources available to you.

If you are experiencing an emergency, please call 911.

Domestic Violence and Intimate Partner Violence
National Domestic Violence Hotline
Hotline: (800) 799-7233

Available 24 hours a day, 7 days a week via phone and online chat. The National Domestic Violence Hotline (The Hotline) is available for anyone experiencing domestic violence, seeking resources or information, or questioning unhealthy aspects of their relationship.

Love is Respect – National Teen Dating Abuse Hotline
Hotline: (866) 331-9474
Text: 22522

Available 24 hours a day, 7 days a week via phone, text, and online chat.
Love is Respect offers information, support, and advocacy to young people who have questions or concerns about their dating relationships.

StrongHearts Native Helpline
Hotline: (844) 762-8483

Available Monday through Friday, 9:00 AM to 5:30 PM CST via phone.
The StrongHearts Native Helpline is a safe, anonymous, and confidential service for Native Americans experiencing domestic violence and dating violence.

Pathways to Safety International
Hotline: (833) 723-3833
Email: crisis@pathwaystosafety.org

Available 24 hours a day, 7 days a week via phone, email, and online chat.
Pathways to Safety International assists Americans experiencing interpersonal and gender-based violence abroad.

Gay, Lesbian, Bisexual and Transgender National Hotline
Hotline: (888) 843-4564
Youth Talkline: (800) 246-7743
Senior Helpline: (888) 234-7243
Email: help@LGBThotline.org

Hours vary, available via phone and online chat.
The LGBT National Help Center serves gay, lesbian, bisexual, transgender, and questioning people by providing free and confidential
peer support and local resources.

Womens Law
Email hotline: https://hotline.womenslaw.org/

The WomensLaw online helpline provides basic legal information,
referrals, and emotional support for victims of abuse.

Sexual Assault
Rape, Abuse, and Incest National Network (RAINN) – National
Sexual Assault Hotline
Hotline: (800) 656-4673

Available 24 hours a day, 7 days a week via phone and online chat.
RAINN (Rape, Abuse & Incest National Network) is the nation's
largest anti-sexual violence organization. RAINN created and operates the National Sexual Assault Hotline (800-656-HOPE, online.
rainn.org y rainn.org/es) in partnership with more than 1,000 local
sexual assault service providers across the country and operates the
DoD Safe Helpline for the Department of Defense. RAINN also

carries out programs to prevent sexual violence, help survivors, and ensure that perpetrators are brought to justice.

<u>Department of Defense (DOD) Safe Helpline for Sexual Assault</u>
Hotline: (877) 995-5247

Available 24 hours a day, 7 days a week via phone and online chat. The DOD Safe Helpline is a crisis support service designed to provide sexual assault services for survivors, their loved ones, and other members of the DOD community.

Human Trafficking
<u>National Human Trafficking Hotline</u>
Hotline: (888) 373-7888 Text: 233733

The National Human Trafficking Hotline is a national anti-trafficking hotline serving victims and survivors of human trafficking and the anti-trafficking community in the United States. The toll-free hotline is available to answer calls from anywhere in the country, 24 hours a day, 7 days a week, every day of the year in more than 200 languages.

Children, Youth, and Teenagers
<u>National Runaway Safeline</u>
Hotline: (800) 786-2929
Email: <u>info@1800runaway.org</u>

Available 24 hours a day, 7 days a week via phone, email, forum, and online chat.
The National Runaway Safeline provides crisis and support services for homeless and runaway youth in the United States.

National Center for Missing and Exploited Children (NCMEC)
Hotline: (800) 843-5678Cyber
Tipline: http://www.missingkids.com/gethelpnow/cybertipline

NCMEC serves as a clearinghouse and comprehensive reporting center for all issues related to the prevention of and recovery from child victimization.

ChildHelp National Child Abuse Hotline
Hotline: (800) 422-4453

Available 24 hours a day, 7 days a week via phone and text.
The ChildHelp National Child Abuse Hotline is dedicated to the prevention of child abuse. Serving the U.S. and Canada, the hotline is staffed 24 hours a day, 7 days a week with professional crisis counselors who—through interpreters—provide assistance in over 170 languages. The hotline offers crisis intervention, information, and referrals to thousands of emergency, social service, and support resources. All calls are confidential.

Boystown USA – Your Life Your Voice Helpline
Hotline: (800) 448-3000
Text: Text VOICE to 20121 (hours vary)

Available 24 hours a day, 7 days a week via phone, email, text, and online chat.
Your Life Your Voice is a program of Boystown USA and is available to children, parents, and families who are struggling with self-harm, mental health disorders, and abuse.

Mental Health and Substance Abuse

<u>National Suicide Prevention Lifeline</u>
Hotline: (800) 273-8255

Available 24 hours a day, 7 days a week via phone and online chat. The National Suicide Prevention Lifeline provides free and confidential support for people in distress, prevention and crisis resources for you or your loved ones, and best practices for professionals.

<u>National Alliance on Mental Illness (NAMI) Helpline</u>
Hotline: (800) 950-6264
Email: <u>info@nami.org</u>

Available Monday through Friday, 10:00am to 6:00pm Eastern Standard Time.
The NAMI Helpline assists individuals and families who have questions about mental health disorders, treatment, and support services.

<u>Substance Abuse and Mental Health Services Administration (SAMHSA) Helpline</u>
Hotline: (800) 662-4357

Available 24 hours a day, 7 days a week via phone in English and Spanish
SAMHSA's National Helpline provides free and confidential treatment referral and information service for individuals and families facing mental and/or substance abuse disorders.